Helion & Company Limited
Unit 8 Amherst Business Centre
Budbrooke Road
Warwick
CV34 5WE
England
Tel. 01926 499 619
Email: info@helion.co.uk
Website: www.helion.co.uk
Twitter: @helionbooks
Visit our blog http://blog.helion.co.uk/

Published by Helion & Company 2022
Designed and typeset by Farr out
    Publications, Wokingham, Berkshire
Cover designed by Paul Hewitt, Battlefield
    Design (www.battlefield-design.co.uk)

Text © Antonio Luis Sapienza Fracchia 2022
Illustrations © as individually credited
Colour profiles © Luca Canossa, Tom Cooper,
    Anderson Subtil and Goran Sudar 2022
Maps drawn by Antonio Luis Sapienza &
    Anderson Subtil © Helion & Company
    2022

ISBN 978-1-915070-74-6

British Library Cataloguing-in-Publication
    Data
A catalogue record for this book is available
    from the British Library

We always welcome receiving book
proposals from prospective authors.

CONTENTS

ACKNOWLEDGEMENTS

The author would like to thank the following individuals and institutions for their precious help: historians Milda Rivarola and the late Adrian English, Cayetano Quatrocchi, Fuerza Aérea Paraguaya, Armada Paraguaya, Ejército Paraguayo, Policía Nacional, Instituto de Historia y Museo Militar del Ministerio de Defensa Nacional.

INTRODUCTION

After the revolution of 1947, Paraguayan society was deeply divided. Many people went into exile, especially to Argentina, and the government continued to be dominated by the Colorado Party, which emerged stronger from the conflict.

President General Higinio Morínigo was deposed in 1948 and a series of governments followed one another until General Alfredo Stroessner came to power in 1954. Opponents soon realised that public freedoms would not be restored, and by the mid-1950s they had begun to plan how to overthrow the government. For his part, Stroessner sought to consolidate his power by strengthening the armed forces, appealing to the American government for help with acquiring weapons, training and attack aircraft.

Although President Eisenhower's administration was determined to help in the fight against communism in Latin America, all Paraguayan requests for arms were rejected with the excuse that Paraguay would not have the funds to pay for them. Nevertheless, the United States maintained a military mission in Paraguay, which advised and trained the Paraguayan Army troops. This would prove very useful during confrontations with guerrillas, first with the group called M14-V (*14 de Mayo*) made up of Liberals and *Febreristas*, and then with the Marxist FULNA (*Frente Unido de Liberación Nacional*, United Front of National Liberation), between 1959 and 1965 in the jungles of Alto Paraná, Caazapá and Itapúa.

The fighting was cruel and bloody. The Paraguayan Army, with the help of the Military Aviation and the Navy, first completely surrounded the M14-V troops, massacring many and capturing others, who were held in military prisons. Against the FULNA, the armed forces were ordered not to take prisoners, since the prevailing mentality at the time was to eliminate all communists. Very few survived to tell the tale. Minor skirmishes continued until the mid-1960s in the mountains of the central region of Paraguay, known as Yvyturusú, until all were captured or eliminated.

Following the failure of both guerrilla groups, a further attempted uprising was made between 1974 and 1976 by the OPM (*Organización Primero de Marzo*, or 1 March Organization), a group of urban guerrillas made up of communists and socialists. However, they were quickly disrupted by the local police. Meanwhile, a plot to assassinate President Stroessner in 1974, led by Dr Agustín Goiburú, was also thwarted by the regime's security forces; everyone involved was arrested, tortured and 'eliminated'.

A final insurrection was known as the 'Caaguazú Case', a group of peasants that in March 1980 tried to protest against the injustices of the regime. The government responded harshly and mobilised 5,000 effectives of the armed forces to hunt the guerrillas, including close air support by armed Air Force helicopters. Most of the group were captured, tortured and later killed.

In September 1980, the former president of Nicaragua, Anastasio Somoza Debayle, who was in exile in Paraguay, was assassinated by a commando group of seven guerrillas belonging to the *Ejército Revolucionario del Pueblo* (ERP, or People's Revolutionary Army) from Argentina, in the service of the Sandinista government in Nicaragua. The action was codenamed Operation Reptile. The last massive repression instigated by Stroessner's regime took place straight after the assassination, but only one ERP effective was captured and killed.

Until 1989, guerrilla operations in Paraguay were very little known, being almost a taboo subject. Only after the coup that overthrew General Stroessner during that year did testimonies by ex-guerrilla members begin to be published, but until now, no author has written (at least in English) about the government's military operations which successfully prevented the installation of a Cuban-style communist regime in Paraguay.

Antonio Luis Sapienza
Asunción, January 2021

1

PARAGUAY'S POLITICAL SITUATION IN THE 1950s AND BEYOND

The political instability in Paraguay of the late 1940s and early 1950s brought a series of short-lived government administrations, all of which were deposed by coups.

Straight after the bloody revolution of 1947, President General Higinio Morínigo remained in power, but was deposed by a coup on 3 June 1948. A civilian, Dr Juan Manuel Frutos, was appointed president just to complete the presidential term, which ended on 15 August that year. Elections had been held in February 1948, with Juan Natalicio González emerging victorious. He started his presidential term in August 1948 but was overthrown by a coup in January the following year. The national congress appointed General Raimundo Rolón, a Chaco War veteran, as a provisional president, but he lasted less than a month in the post. Felipe Molas López then became the new *de facto* president with the intention of completing the 1948–53 presidential term, but once again he was deposed by a coup, this time in September 1949. The congress then appointed Federico Chaves as the new president, and he was finally able to complete the 1948–53 term. In the 1953 elections, Chaves was elected president of the Republic, to serve from 1953–58.

Although Chaves was married, he had a mistress, Isabel Vallejos, who was a widow. She started manipulating the president for her own purposes, and within a few months Chaves was essentially a puppet leader, the real power being in the hands of Vallejos. So evident was this that civil and military authorities, and even diplomats, visited her home instead of the Government Palace for various reasons, such as to get a promotion or to start a lucrative business. She was the 'power behind the throne', which caused great distress to many people, among them the Commander-in-Chief of the armed forces, General Alfredo Stroessner. There were many cases of indiscipline in the armed forces, and several different groups within the Colorado Party started disputing for power. Inflation was high and access to essential goods such as flour, sugar and beef became a luxury. Many products were rationed and people had to stay in line for hours to obtain a state voucher for these goods. Meanwhile, the former president of the Central Bank, Epifanio Mendez Fleitas, a prominent figure in the Colorado Party, was conspiring against the government, and there were also rumours of an imminent coup. General Stroessner therefore decided to act.

On 4 May 1954, military forces commanded by Stroessner besieged the capital Asunción and attacked the Police Headquarters to gain control of the government. The president sought refuge in the Military School building, but the commander there, Brigadier

General Alfredo Stroessner, Commander-in-Chief of the Paraguayan armed forces during the Chavez administration, led a coup in 1954 and later became the President of Paraguay. (Instituto de Historia y Museo Militar del Ministerio de Defensa Nacional)

The presidents of Paraguay between 1940 and 1954. From left to right: General Higinio Morínigo (1940–48), Dr Juan Manuel Frutos (1948), Juan Natalicio González (1948–49), General Raimundo Rolón (1949), Dr Felipe Molas López (1949) and Federico Chavez (1949–54). (Instituto de Historia y Museo Militar del MDN)

General Marcial Samaniego, was loyal to Stroessner and kept Chaves as prisoner; his only option was to resign. The Colorado Party then appointed its own president, Tomás Romero Pereira, as the provisional president of Paraguay while a consensus candidate was being searched for. At that moment, there were no strong civilian candidates, so they offered the presidency to the 41-year-old Alfredo Stroessner. When elections were held on 11 July, Stroessner was the only candidate. He officially became the president of the country on 15 August 1954, to complete the 1953–58 presidential term. In 1956, Stroessner signed a decree promoting himself to the highest rank in the armed forces, General of the Army (four-star general).

From the start, Stroessner defined himself as an extreme anti-communist leader, which was perfect for the US government's National Security Doctrine during the Cold War. Paraguay was at that time a very poor country; most of the population – almost 1.4 million people – did not have access to educational and health services. There was less than 100km of paved roads in the country, no national airline, a very poor merchant navy, running tap water was non-existent, there was a very inefficient electric power system for only a few neighbourhoods in the capital and basic goods were scarce, among countless other problems.

Stroessner fulfilled his promises to pacify the country, achieve greater financial stability and modernise the infrastructure. He obtained the support of businessmen and landowners to achieve political and economic stability, and above all to attract foreign investment. Starting in the mid-1950s, his government focused on huge public works under the motto 'Peace and Work', the projects financed by a series of loans from the Eximbank and the Development Loan Fund of the United States. Between 1960 and 1980, Paraguay received more than a billion dollars in loans from the American government. The first huge project was a running tap water system for the capital and the country's other main cities. This was followed by the construction of more paved roads, first of all to Stroessner's hometown of Encarnación, then to the east towards the Brazilian border, where a new city was built in the middle of the forests, appropriately named Puerto Presidente Stroessner. Construction of the Trans Chaco Road was initiated, as well as roads to the north to the cities of Concepción and Pedro Juan Caballero. All electricity, water and telephone services were nationalised, as well as the railroad system. As in all dictatorship regimes, streets, avenues, towns, schools, squares, bridges and even Asunción International Airport were named after the nation's leader.

On 4 May 1958, the Vice President of the United States, Richard Nixon, visited Paraguay. His visit served to reinforce US support for 'their man' in Paraguay, within the hemispheric security policy, in the struggle against Soviet expansionism. Nixon opened a CIA office at the American Embassy in Asunción and had a meeting with General Stroessner, who had met President Eisenhower in Panama in 1956.

In 1958, Stroessner was elected for a further five-year period, and re-elected again in 1963. One of the key successes of Stroessner's regime was the appointment of loyal military friends as ministers in his government, especially in the Treasury, the Interior Ministry, the police, the public works and communications departments and of course the Defence Ministry. Most of those appointed were veterans of the Chaco War against Bolivia. The Stroessner regime's foundations relied on two huge pillars: the armed forces and the Colorado Party. Geopolitically, Stroessner's regime moved closer not only to the United States but also to Brazil, and later to Taiwan and South Africa, while edging away from Argentina.

Between 1954 and 1960, when Stroessner faced his greatest national and international threats, Washington's political, economic and military support was essential for the survival and consolidation of the regime. Besides other fields of cooperation between the two countries such as health, agriculture, cattle raising, education, infrastructure modernisation and financial stabilisation, military aid was very important, especially in the fight against communism.

US president Dwight Eisenhower's administration sent arms to Paraguay and increased the number of military advisers in Asunción. As referred to above, Paraguayan Army, Navy and Air Force officers and NCOs received anti-subversive training in several American military establishments. All such aid was channelled through the American Embassy in Asunción, whose ambassadors – retired Vice Admiral Arthur A. Ageton (1954–57), William Ploeser (1957–59) and Harry F. Stimpson (1959–61) – played a decisive role in strengthening bilateral ties.

Regarding political parties in Paraguay, the two main players were the centrist Liberal Party (PL), which was originally founded under the name of the Democratic Centre on 10 July 1887, and the conservative Republican National Association (The Colorado Party) (ANR/PC), which was founded on 11 September 1887. The Paraguayan Communist Party (PCP), obviously Marxist, was founded on 19 February 1928 and the centre-left Revolutionary Febrerista Party (PRF) had its origins in the revolution of 1936 but was officially founded on 11 December 1951 in exile in Buenos Aires, Argentina. On 15 May 1960, the Christian Democratic Party (PDC), also centre-left, was officially founded.

The Colorado Party ruled the country from 1887–1904, being displaced by the Liberal Party after the revolution of 1904. From that year to 1936, several Liberal governments ruled the country, then straight after the Chaco War, a revolutionary army movement known as the Febreristas or Franquistas (their leader was Colonel Rafael Franco, a Chaco War veteran) overthrew the Liberals and was briefly in government but was deposed by the Army a year-and-a-half later. The Liberal Party returned to government until the death of the president, General José Félix Estigarribia in 1940. Estigarribia´s successor, General Higinio Morínigo, ruled with the help of the Colorado Party and outlawed the Liberal Party. In 1947, a coalition of the Liberal, Febrerista and Communist parties tried to overthrow Morínigo's government through a bloody revolution but were unsuccessful. From then on, the Colorado Party continued to rule the country, consolidating its power through the armed forces, which were fully affiliated to the ruling party.

2

THE PARAGUAYAN ARMED FORCES IN THE 1950s AND BEYOND

Army

In the 1950s, the Paraguayan Army had a total of around 10,000 effectives. It was organised in five Military Regions (RM), as follows:

- RM I (HQ Asunción)
- RM II (HQ Villarrica)
- RM III (HQ San Juan Bautista)
- RM IV (HQ Concepción)
- RM V (HQ Puerto Presidente Stroessner)

The Chaco region, west of the Paraguay River, corresponding to the former RM V, was then designated the Chaco Military Territory with its HQ in the city of Mariscal Estigarribia.

The Army components of each Military Region were as follows:

- Infantry Division Nr. 1 (HQ Asunción), with Infantry Regiment Nr. 14 *Cerro Corá* as its major permanent element.
- Infantry Division Nr. 2 (HQ Villarrica), with Infantry Regiment Nr. 27 *General Garay* as its major permanent element.
- Infantry Division Nr. 3 (HQ San Juan Bautista), with Infantry Regiment Nr. 8 *Piribebuy* as its major permanent element.
- Infantry Division Nr. 4 (HQ Concepción), with Infantry Regiment Nr. 5 *General Diaz* as its major permanent element.
- Infantry Division Nr. 5 (HQ Puerto Presidente Stroessner), with Infantry Regiment Nr. 15 *Lomas Valentinas* as its major permanent element.

The Chaco Military Territory now also hosted the nucleus of a division, the Infantry Division Nr. 6 (HQ Mariscal Estigarribia), with Infantry Regiment Nr. 6 *Boquerón* as its major permanently embodied element.

Although in peacetime each division consisted essentially only of a headquarters and a single infantry regiment, upon mobilisation, each was scheduled to expand to three regiments, with small integral cavalry, engineer and logistic elements but without organic artillery support.

Remaining outside the territorial organisation, Cavalry Division Nr. 1 (with its HQ still at Campo Grande, Asunción) – now including Cavalry Regiment Nr. 4 *Acá Carayá* in addition to Cavalry Regiment Nr. 1 *Valois Rivarola*, Cavalry Regiment Nr. 2 *General Toledo*, Cavalry Regiment Nr. 3 *Coronel Mongelós*, plus a small mechanised element and with some integral artillery support – remained the major tactical manoeuvre element in peacetime. At Army level there was also the Presidential Escort Battalion, which now become a full regiment, also with small

armoured and artillery elements, plus Artillery Regiment Nr. 1 *General Bruguez*, Sappers Regiment Nr. 1 *General Aquino*, which had become the Army Engineer Command, and the still unnamed Signals Regiment.

This reorganisation involved the resuscitation of the traditional Infantry Division Nr. 1 and Infantry Division Nr. 2 – although these were now renumbered Infantry Division Nr. 6 and Infantry Division Nr. 4, respectively – and the mobilisation of two additional infantry regiments and one cavalry regiment, Infantry Regiment Nr. 8 *Piribebuy*, Infantry Regiment Nr. 15 *Lomas Valentinas* and Cavalry Regiment Nr. 4 *Acá Carayá*, to make a total of at least six permanently embodied infantry regiments and four cavalry regiments, together

Paraguayan Army infantry troops during a parade in the late 1950s. Note the American M1 helmets and the Mauser rifles with bayonets. (Instituto de Historia y Museo Militar del MDN)

Paraguayan Army cavalry officers during a parade in the late 1950s. (Milda Rivarola Archives)

Paraguayan Army Military Police effectives receiving instruction in the late 1950s. (Instituto de Historia y Museo Militar del MDN)

Army sappers crossing a river during manoeuvres in the late 1950s. (Ejército Paraguayo)

General Stroessner addressing high-ranking officers in the Commander-in-Chief's office during a formal lunch in the late 1950s. (Instituto de Historia y Museo Militar del MDN)

with the Presidential Escort Regiment, the sole active group of Artillery Regiment Nr. 1 *General Bruguez*, the five battalions of the Engineer Command and the single battalion of the Signals Regiment. A new type of unit, the frontier battalion, of which there were initially two (Nr. 1 in RM III and Nr. 2 in RM V), had begun to appear and replace the independent infantry battalions, a development which was to presage a functional separation of the Army's territorial defence and tactical manoeuvre elements. On 18 April 1958, the infantry battalion stationed in RM II was designated Infantry Regiment Nr. 27 *General Eugenio Alejandrino Garay*. This raised the number of permanently embodied infantry regiments to four – Nr. 5 *General Díaz*, Nr. 6 *Boquerón*, Nr. 14 *Cerro Corá* and Nr. 27 *General Garay* – plus the existing three cavalry, one artillery, one engineer and one signals regiments. There was also a Presidential Escort Battalion (REP, established in 1949) and at least two independent infantry battalions (one each in RM III and RM V).

The Army Health Corps had three air ambulances – a Beechcraft B35 Bonanza, a Cessna 180 and a Cessna 185 – all of them acquired locally between 1950 and 1962.

Argentina and Brazil had begun to assiduously court successive Paraguayan governments from the early 1950s onwards, both countries presenting quantities of second-hand military equipment to the Paraguayan Army. As tanks (used only by Bolivia and in very small numbers) had performed badly in the Chaco War, the Paraguayan Army had shown little enthusiasm for armour, and its cavalry elements had hitherto remained entirely horsed.

From the mid-1950s onwards, United States military aid also increased, being confined mainly to the provision of transport and communications equipment, although some M101 105mm howitzers, M1A1 40mm anti-aircraft guns, M20 75mm RCLs (recoilless rifles) and quantities of heavy M2 and M30 4.2-inch mortars were also received. M1 Garand rifles were donated in great numbers too, becoming the main troop armament together with the Chaco War-era Mauser rifles and ammunition and a huge stock of M1 helmets.

The president of Paraguay, Army General Alfredo Stroessner, was the Commander-in-Chief of all the Paraguayan armed forces, with Major General Leodegar Cabello as the Army General Chief of Staff.

Officers of the Army, Navy and Air Force graduated from the Military School, which was located in central Asunción, after four years of military education. Once officers, and when they reached the rank of captain or major, they went to the School of War for two years. There were several schools in the three branches of the armed forces for Non-Commissioned Officers (NCOs) with various specialties, where they studied for two or three years. Many of them received scholarships to study in the Military School to become officers.

There was a permanent US Military Mission in Paraguay (US Army Attaché, USARMA), with a number of advisers who were training Army officers and NCOs. In 1960, the USARMA was led by US Army General Beverly Jones. There was also a Brazilian Army Military Mission for troop training.

In 1965, Paraguay contributed a unit to the Inter American peacekeeping force during the civil war in the Dominican Republic, and since then has contributed contingents of varying size to disaster relief and peacekeeping forces worldwide, mainly under the auspices of the United Nations, with an engineer unit in Haiti at the time of writing.

From the mid-1960s onwards, United States military aid had also increased, MAP (Military Assistance Programme) deliveries to Paraguay including 54 M1918A2 Browning Automatic

Paraguayan military commanders with President Stroessner in the late 1950s. From left to right: Brigadier Generals Sarubbi and Grenno, Major General Barrientos, Brigadier General Morínigo, General Stroessner, Brigadier General Coscia, Rear Admiral Pereira Saguier, and Major Generals Cáceres and Brítez. (Ejército Paraguayo)

Army privates being trained in the use of radio equipment in the late 1950s. (Ejército Paraguayo)

Rifles and 30,749 M1 Garand rifles, between 1964–66 and 1964–74 respectively. A further 338 M1919A4 light machine guns and three M2HB heavy machine guns were received between 1965 and 1976, together with 27 M79 grenade launchers, which were acquired between 1966 and 1968. Six M20 75mm RCLs were also received in 1965, followed by an unspecified number of older M18 57mm RLs in 1966. Twenty-five 3.5-inch RLs were obtained between 1968 and 1976, while 13 US 81mm mortars were acquired between 1964 and 1969.

Despite the considerable quantities of Chaco War-vintage equipment still in service, more modern artillery pieces were a pressing requirement, and artillery (among other things) was requested by Stroessner when he met US president Lyndon Johnson in 1967. Presumably as a result of this, 12 75mm M116

pack howitzers were received from the US in 1968, while a similar number of M2A1 105mm howitzers were transferred to Paraguay by the US between the late 1960s and 1980. Several M20 75mm RCLs and quantities of M2 and M30 4.2-inch heavy mortars were also received during this period.

The FN FAL rifle also began to be adopted generally during the mid-1970s, gradually replacing the venerable Mauser as the standard small arm for Paraguayan troops.

Argentina and Brazil continued to consolidate their influence in Paraguay with the transfer of mainly obsolete defence equipment. This included six 75mm/L40 Bofors field guns, received from Argentina in 1970, followed by six more in 1979 and between four and six Mk VIII Vickers 6-inch mobile coastal guns from Brazil, which is also reported to have transferred up to 12 75mm Krupp M37 or M38 field guns to Paraguay during the 1970s.

In November 1980, two additional infantry divisions (Infantry Division Nr. 7 at Campo Jurado and Infantry Division Nr. 8 at Mayor Lagerenza, both in the Chaco) were created and the Army was reorganised into three Army Corps, as follows:

- I Army Corps (HQ Asunción), comprising:
  ◊ Infantry Division Nr. 1 (HQ Asunción), with Infantry Regiment Nr. 14 *Cerro Corá* as its major permanent element
  ◊ Infantry Division Nr. 3 (HQ San Juan Bautista), with Infantry Regiment Nr. 8 *Piribebuy* as its major permanent element
  ◊ Cavalry Division Nr. 1 (HQ Campo Grande), with Cavalry Regiment Nr. 1 *Valois Rivarola*, Cavalry Regiment Nr. 2 *General Toledo*, Cavalry Regiment Nr. 3 *Coronel Mongelós* and Cavalry Regiment Nr. 4 *Acá Carayá* as its major elements
- II Army Corps (HQ Villarica), comprising:
  ◊ Infantry Division Nr. 2 (HQ Villarica), with Infantry Regiment Nr. 27 *General Garay* as its major permanent element
  ◊ Infantry Division Nr. 4 (HQ Concepción), with Infantry Regiment Nr. 5 *General Díaz* as its major permanent element
  ◊ Infantry Division Nr. 5 (HQ Puerto Presidente Stroessner), with Infantry Regiment Nr. 15 *Lomas Valentinas* as its major permanent element
- III Army Corps (HQ Mariscal Estigarribia), comprising:
  ◊ Infantry Division Nr. 6 (HQ Mcal. Estigarribia), with Infantry Regiment Nr. 6 *Boquerón* as its major permanent element
  ◊ Infantry Division Nr. 7 (HQ Campo Jurado), with Infantry Regiment Nr. 10 *Sauce* as its major permanent element
  ◊ Infantry Division Nr. 8 (HQ Mayor Lagerenza), with Infantry Regiment Nr. 4 *Curupayty* as its major permanent element

The Presidential Escort Regiment (now consisting of an infantry battalion, a military police battalion and small armoured and artillery elements, equipped respectively with the country's only heavy tanks, three ex-Argentine Sherman Fireflies, three M9 halftracks and two M2A1 105mm howitzers), Artillery Regiment Nr. 1 *General Bruguez* (which now became the Army Artillery Command and expanded to three groups) and Army Engineer Command (which had acquired

a sixth battalion in 1971), together with the Signals Regiment, remained as Army-level units. Infantry Regiment Nr. 16 *Mariscal López*, which functioned as a garrison unit at the important military centre of Paraguarí, had also been mobilised in 1980 and although an infantry unit, formed part of the Army Artillery Command.

The number of permanently embodied infantry regiments therefore now rose to nine, by virtue of the mobilisation of Infantry Regiment Nr. 4 *Curupayty* and Infantry Regiment Nr. 10 *Sauce*, although most of the infantry regiments still had only a single battalion, consisting of an HQ, two rifle companies and a heavy weapons company.

Regarding armoured vehicles of the Paraguayan Army, in 1969 the American government donated nine M3A1 Stuart light tanks. Two years later, in 1971, Argentina donated the first three Sherman Firefly tanks, followed by another three in 1981. In 1988, three Fireflies were returned to Argentina in exchange for three Shermans with diesel engines and a 105mm gun. For its part, Brazil donated 12 M3A1 Stuart light tanks and 12 M2 and M5 halftrack vehicles with diesel engines, some of them equipped with 20mm anti-aircraft guns.

Air Force
With some 850 effectives in the Paraguayan Air Force (*Fuerza Aérea Paraguaya*, FAP), most of the Lend-Lease aircraft donated by the American government between 1942 and 1945 were still on strength at the beginning of the 1950s. They consisted of a large number of Fairchild PT-19 primary trainers, Vultee BT-13 basic trainers, just three armed North American AT-6C Texan advanced trainers and a pair of Beechcraft UC-45F transport trainers. During the 1950s, very few acquisitions were made for the air arm. Between 1949 and 1957, five Beechcraft 35 Bonanza light aircraft were purchased. Then in 1953, a Douglas DC-3 transport was acquired in the US, followed by four C-47s and two PBY-5A Catalinas in 1955 for the Military Air Transport (TAM), which was created in 1954. In 1955, the first two helicopters were bought, two brand-new Bell 47G.2s. In the following year, six Brazilian-built versions of the Fairchild PT-19 primary trainer called Galeão PT-3FG were acquired, plus eight more in 1959. In 1958, a single Beechcraft AT-11 Kansan bombing trainer was purchased, while a Cessna 180 was acquired locally in 1961.

In 1953, the Paraguayan government made a request to Colonel Sydney T. Smith, chief of the US Military Air Mission in Paraguay, to purchase 20 armed North American AT-6D Texans, plus four Bell 47G.2s and four Beechcraft Bonanzas, for $2 million. However, this order was not fulfilled due to lack of funds by the Paraguayan government.

A long line of M3A1 Stuart light tanks (left) and a pair of M4A1 Sherman tanks (right) during parades in the mid-1970s. (Instituto de Historia y Museo Militar del MDN)

Commanders of the Paraguayan Air Arm between 1953 and 1969, from left to right, Colonel DEM (Chief of Staff) Epifanio Ovando (1953–56), General Juan Antonio Cáceres (1953–62) and General Adrián Jara (1962–69). (Fuerza Aérea Paraguaya)

Paraguayan Air Arm Galeão PT-3FG (Brazilian-built Fairchild PT-19) primary trainers at Ñu-Guazú AFB in the late 1950s. (Fuerza Aérea Paraguaya)

Paraguayan Air Force Vultee BT-13A basic trainers at Ñu-Guazú AFB in the late 1940s. (Instituto de Historia y Museo Militar del MDN)

A Paraguayan Air Force North American AT-6C Texan advance trainer, also used in light attack roles, flying over Ñu-Guazú AFB in the late 1940s. (Instituto de Historia y Museo Militar del MDN)

In November 1955, the Paraguayan government once again made a formal request to its US counterpart for the acquisition of 20 armed North American AT-6D/Gs plus 10 replacement engines and other parts for maintenance for three years. As before, the order was not fulfilled because of lack of funds.

In November 1958, the Paraguayan Ministry of Foreign Affairs presented an official document to the American Embassy requesting the acquisition of the following airplanes for the air arm: six Lockheed T-33 jet trainers, one Douglas C-47, six Douglas C-54s (both transports), two armed North American B-25 or two Martin B-26 bombers, 15 trainers – including Fairchild PT-19s, BT-13s, AT-6s, one Beechcraft C-45 and four Beechcraft 35 Bonanzas – as well as tools, spare parts and engines. However, nothing came out of this request.

Only in 1962 was Paraguay included in the list of the MAP for the donation of transport aircraft, mainly for the Military Air Transport, and later some light trainers. The first donation in 1962 consisted of two Douglas C-47s, with four more in 1964. In 1962, an Army Cessna 180 was transferred to the Air Force and Brazil donated a single armed North American AT-6D Texan. Between 1963 and 1967, the air arm also received five Cessna 185/U-17s through the MAP. Argentina donated a De Havilland DH-104 Dove to be used as a presidential plane in 1962, and the following year four Neiva 56B Paulistinha L-6 basic trainers were acquired from Brazil. During the 1960s and until the mid-1970s, the American government donated a number of aircraft through the MAP: Douglas C-47s (five in 1967, five in 1970, three in 1973 and one in 1974); eight Bell OH-13Hs in 1972; five Cessna T-41Bs in 1974; four and 1976, Brazil donated 12 armed North American T-6Ds Texans, 17 North American T-6Gs and three Douglas DC-6Bs. Regarding trainers, eight Brazilian-built Fokker S.11/T-21s were purchased in 1972 and eight Aerotec T-23 Uirapurús in 1975. In 1979, the government of Paraguay ordered the purchase of nine Embraer EMB-326GB/AT-26 Xavante jets, plus one more sample in 1980. In the same year, South Africa donated 15 NorthAmerican T-6G Texans.

A Paraguayan Air Arm Neiva 56b/L-6 Paulistinha trainer at Ñu-Guazú AFB in the early 1960s. (General Ret. Alcibiades Soto Velleau)

The Air Force's regular air service, the *Transporte Aéreo Militar* (TAM, Military Air Transport), had flights to the main cities of Paraguay from 1954, using Douglas C-47s. Meanwhile, the state-owned LATN (*Líneas Aéreas de Transporte Nacional*) operated a fleet of Beech Bonanza, Beech C-45, Noorduyn Norseman and PBY-5A Catalina aircraft to complement TAM services.

A Paraguayan Air Force Military Air Transport Douglas DC-3 at Asunción International Airport in the mid-1950s. (Fuerza Aérea Paraguaya)

Although too late to participate in the fight against the guerrillas, the Paraguayan Air Force activated a paratrooper regiment, the *Silvio Pettirossi*, in 1966. That same year, the Transport and Training Air Group (*Grupo Aéreo de Entrenamiento y Transporte*, GAET) was created, with a training squadron and a transport squadron. From 1953–56, the commander was Colonel Epifanio Ovando, and he was succeeded by Major General Juan Antonio Cáceres (1956–62) and Brigadier General Adrián Jara (1962–69). Brigadier General Vicente Quiñonez was the FAP commander between 1969 and 1977, being replaced by Major General Luis González Ravetti (1977–88).

Paraguayan Air Arm Beechcraft AT-11 Kansan. Note how the nose was modified locally. (Fuerza Aérea Paraguaya)

There was also a US Military Air Mission in Paraguay, whose advisers trained FAP officers and NCOs. The mission had a USAF Douglas C-47 stationed in the country which was also used to train DC-3/C-47 crews for the TAM. Several air arm officers and NCOs were also sent to the US and the Panama Canal Zone to take various courses, including pilot training and maintenance. The air mission

De Havilland Canada DHC-2 Beavers in 1975; and one Convair C-131D Samaritan in 1976.

In 1968, a brand-new De Havilland Canada DHC-6-200 Twin Otter was acquired to be used as a presidential plane. The Argentine government donated three Douglas DC-3s in 1969 and a De Havilland Canada DHC-3 Otter in 1971. Between 1972

A Paraguayan Air Force Beechcraft A35 Bonanza in the mid-1950s. (Fuerza Aérea Paraguaya)

Effectives of the Airborne Regiment *Silvio Pettirossi* of the FAP posing next to a TAM C-47 before a practice jump in the mid-1960s. (Fuerza Aérea Paraguaya)

Four Douglas C-47s were received through the Military Assistance Programme (MAP) in 1964. (FAP)

The Paraguayan Air Force commander, Colonel Epifanio Ovando (left), being received by personnel at Albrook Air Force Station (Panama Canal Zone) during a visit in the mid-1950s. (Col. Agustín Pasmor Archives)

Paraguayan Air Arm Bell 47G.2 in the late 1950s. Two presidents are on board, Juscelino Kubitschek (Brazil) and Alfredo Stroessner (Paraguay), during a summit in Foz do Iguaçu, Brazil. (Kubitschek Archives)

A USAF Douglas C-47 of the US Military Air Mission to Paraguay. (via Dan Hagedorn)

A Military Air Transport Douglas C-47 taxiing on the then recently built airstrip at Puerto Presidente Stroessner, Alto Paraná, in the late 1950s. (Fuerza Aérea Paraguaya)

Paraguayan Air Force trainers in the 1970s: a Fokker S.11/T-21 (left) and Aerotec T-23 Uirapurú (right). (Fuerza Aérea Paraguaya & Peter Steinemann)

The first jets to enter service in the Paraguayan Air Force were Embraer EMB-326GB/AT-26 Xavantes in 1979–80. (Embraer)

was closed down in 1976 and the US military aid to Paraguay ceased during President Jimmy Carter's administration.

Navy

In the late 1950s, the Paraguayan Navy had around 1,000 effectives and a total of 20 vessels, including two armed gunboats – the Chaco War veteran twin ships *Paraguay* and *Humaitá* – three armed patrol vessels (*Capitán Cabral*, *Coronel Martínez* and *Tte. Herreros*), the buoy tender *Capitán Figari*, the flat boat *Tacuary* (which had been a gunboat during the Chaco War), the freighters *Mcal. Estigarribia*, *Presidente Stroessner* and *Bahía Negra*, the transport ship *Teniente Pratts Gill*, the dredges *Progreso* and *Tte. Oscar Carreras Saguier*, and

Various FAP transport aircraft. Clockwise, a De Havilland Canada DHC-2/L-20 Beaver, De Havilland Canada DHC-3 Otter, Convair C-131D Samaritan and Douglas DC-6B. (Fuerza Aérea Paraguaya, Dan Hagedorn, Horacio Gareiso & Aparecido Camazano A.)

the survey boat *Suboficial Rogelio Lesme*. There were also six small picket boats, designated P-1 to P-6, donated by the US government in 1944, and two patrol motorboats built locally in 1960.

In 1964, the Argentine Navy donated a minesweeper, which was christened the *Nanawa*. Two more would follow in 1968, the *Capitán Meza* and *Teniente Fariña*. In 1965, the US government donated a tug, a floating dry dock and a floating workshop. Between 1967 and

1971, six Sewart Type 701 patrol craft were received. In 1968, the Paraguayan Navy incorporated a cargo ship, the *Guaraní*, which was built in Spain. Besides carrying cargo between European ports and Paraguay, it was also used as a school vessel to train Paraguayan Navy crews in sea navigation. In 1970, two LCU-501-class landing craft were donated by the US. Two years later, the Argentine Navy donated a former US Navy LSM-1-class landing ship, which was

Paraguayan Navy commanders between 1949 and 1976, from left to right, Rear Admiral Gabriel A. Patiño (1949–56), Rear Admiral Benito Pereira Saguier (1956–66) and Vice Admiral Hugo González (1966–76). (Armada Paraguaya)

LATIN AMERICA@WAR VOLUME 27

The Paraguayan Navy twin gunboats *Paraguay* (C.1) and *Humaitá* (C.2) at Sajonia Naval Base in Asunción. (Adrian English)

The Paraguayan Navy minesweeper ARP *Nanawa* M.1 (later P.02) in the 1960s. (Armada Paraguaya)

ARP *Boquerón* B.C.1 in the mid-1970s. (Armada Paraguaya)

A Paraguayan Naval Aviation NAF N3N-3 at Sajonia NAS in the late 1950s. (Aviación Naval Paraguaya)

A Paraguayan Naval Aviation Republic RC-3 Seabee at Asunción International Airport in the early 1960s. (Alex Reinhard)

converted into a helicopter carrier and christened the *Boquerón* by the Paraguayan Navy. In 1974, a further tugboat was received from the US.

There was also a tiny Naval Aviation with two Naval Aircraft Factory N3N-3 floatplanes, which were donated by the US Lend-Lease programme in 1943, plus three Republic RC-3 Seabee, two

Grumman JRF-5 Goose and three Vultee BT-13 basic trainers. In 1966, the Naval Aviation started a regular air service for passengers, mail and small cargo under the name of the Naval Air Service (*Servicio Aero Naval*, SAN), with two Grumman JRF-5 Goose amphibians, which departed from Sajonia Naval Base in Asunción to various ports on the Paraguay River. It the mid-1960s, it also received

A Paraguayan Naval Aviation Vultee BT-13A, still with its Argentine Naval Aviation colours,
flying over the Paraguay River in 1960. (Aviación Naval Paraguaya)

Members of the Argentine Navy Military Mission in Paraguay
being greeted by the Paraguayan Navy commander
and other naval officers at Asunción International
Airport in the early 1960s. (Armada Paraguaya)

Paraguayan Navy NCOs in a military parade in
the late 1950s. (Milda Rivarola Archives)

Paraguayan Navy officers on board the gunboat
Paraguay in the early 1960s. (Armada Paraguaya)

a pair of JRF-6B Goose aircraft from the Argentine Naval Mission
in Paraguay. Two Cessna U206As were received in 1966, then two
U206Cs in 1970. In 1969, two North American T-6s were donated
by the Argentine Naval Aviation. A Cessna 210G was acquired
locally in 1974, while two new Cessna 150Ms were purchased as
basic trainers in 1976. In 1972, the Naval Aviation received four Bell
OH-13Hs through the MAP. In 1979, the Argentine Naval Aviation
donated a Douglas C-47.

The commander of the Paraguayan Navy from 1949–56 was
Rear Admiral Gabriel A. Patiño, who was followed by Rear Admiral
Benito Pereira Saguier (1956–66), Vice Admiral Hugo González
(1966–76) and Vice Admiral César Cortese (1976–87).

An Argentine Naval Mission in Paraguay was led by a vice admiral
and trained Paraguayan Navy officers and NCOs and included an
Air Section with a Grumman JRF-6B Goose that provided training
to naval pilots and mechanics.

Paraguayan Navy Armed Patrol Vessel *Capitán Cabral* (A.1) in the late 1950s. (Armada Paraguaya)

Police

In 1955, the United States contributed to the creation of the Political Intelligence Service of the Ministry of the Interior by sending an expert in anti-communist affairs, US Army Colonel Robert Thierry, as an 'adviser' to provide training and technical support to the Paraguayan police. Stroessner's government also sent police officers to the International Police Academy in Washington for training in counterinsurgency methods. The Paraguayan police also received ammunition, small arms and communication equipment from the American government. The then Chief of the Paraguayan Police and later Minister of the Interior, Edgar L. Ynsfrán, was a very regular visitor to the American Embassy in Asunción, where he exchanged intelligence information with the Americans. Besides the Minister of the Interior, the Police Inspector Commissioners involved in the interrogations of captured guerrillas were Dr Antonio Campos Alúm, Bachen, Juan Arturo Hellman, Raúl Riveros Taponier,

Police officers and detectives posing in front of a Police station in Asunción in the late 1950s. (Policía Nacional)

Garcete, Duarte and Ranulfo López. These were helped by several Police Mayors from various towns and cities of the interior of the country. The only police officers who were involved in search and combat patrols against the subversives were members of the Police Security Guard.

Police officers graduated from the Police School after four years of studies. Police NCOs had their own school, where they studied for two years.

In total, the military and police aid provided by the American government between 1954 and 1959 reached the sum of $10 million, plus another

Paraguayan police officers with salacot helmets in the late 1950s. (Milda Rivarola Archives)

President General Alfredo Stroessner (left) with the Chief of the Paraguayan Police, Dr Edgar L. Ynsfrán (right), in the late 1950s. (Policía Nacional)

Major General Alcibiades Brítez Borges (centre, wearing military uniform) became the Chief of the Police in May 1966, replacing Brigadier General Ramón Duarte Vera. General Brítez is shown visiting the premises of the Police Cooperative that year. (Policía Nacional)

Paraguayan police Academy cadets in the late 1950s. (Policía Nacional)

The Chief of the Paraguayan Police, General Brítez Borges (third from the left in the front row), with high-ranking police officers saluting the flag on national Police Day, 30 August 1973. (Policía Nacional)

Police officers in the Cordillera region checking the mobilisation plan for the festivities of the Virgin of Caacupé in early December 1973. (Policía Nacional)

When Dr Edgar L. Ynsfrán (fourth from the left at the table) was appointed as Minister of the Interior, the then Army Colonel Ramón Duarte Vera (fourth from the right, standing) became the Chief of the Police. Several police officers are shown at the back. (Policía Nacional)

$5 million between 1959 and 1961, the years when the Paraguayan government was fighting the guerrillas. The aid included trucks, small arms, ammunition, light artillery and training.

Between 1962 and 1969, 400 military officers of the Paraguayan Army, Navy and Air Force received counterinsurgency training in several military schools and academies in the United States and in the Panama Canal Zone.

The Police Headquarters building in Asunción (left) in the mid-1960s. (Policía Nacional)

3

THE M14-V GROUP

The first attempt to overthrow Stroessner took place on 4 November 1956, when a coup was planned by several Liberal Party leaders in exile through a group of youngsters who were drafted for military service in the Chaco region. Chaco War veterans and former Army officers also participated in that attempt, including former Captain Juan Bartolomé Araujo, one of the revolutionaries in 1947, ex-Captain Luis Parra and former Colonel Alfredo Ramos, all of them in exile in Argentina, who entered the country clandestinely. Once the government became aware of the plan, the officers fled to Argentina and many young leaders of the Liberal and Febrerista parties were captured and imprisoned in various forts in the Chaco region. Several officials of these political parties were also arrested, along with some leaders of the then-illegal Paraguayan Communist Party, who spent decades in jail.

International events that inspired many young Paraguayans, whether in exile or in their home country, to rebel included the overthrow of the Venezuelan dictator General Marcos Pérez Jiménez, a close friend of Stroessner, and Fulgencio Batista in Cuba. One aspect of the Cuban Revolution led by Fidel Castro that particularly encouraged many Paraguayan opposition politicians was the fact that a small group of guerrillas was able to get the population to rise up and overthrow a hated dictatorship in a short period of time. The Liberal, Febrerista and Communist leaders consequently came to the simple but ill-judged conclusion that if they followed the same Cuban method, they could overthrow Stroessner. However, their simplistic comparison forgot the great differences in the political situation of the two countries. While in Cuba there was already an extensive network of opposition activists within the country who were willing to help the revolutionaries, in Paraguay there were none, and this turned out to be a crucial factor during the failed operations of both the M14-V Group and the FULNA.

The most radical factions of the Liberal and Febrerista parties thus formed the 14 de Mayo movement (M14-V), the Paraguayan Communist Party acting similarly to create the FULNA, both being armed guerrilla organisations.

Chaco War veterans Colonel (Ret.) Alfredo Ramos, who also participated in the revolution of 1947, and Captain (Ret.) Modesto Ramírez were two of the founding members of the M14-V group. (Instituto de Historia y Museo Militar del MDN)

In 1958 there were two attempted armed incursions from Argentina, led by opponents in exile who were mostly retired officers of the Paraguayan Army, some of them veterans of the Chaco War and the revolution of 1947. These former military personnel would join the M14-V in the following year.

At dawn on 1 April 1958, a small armed group linked to the Febrerista Party, commanded by Lieutenants Corazón Chamorro and José Prieto, crossed the Paraná River and attacked the police station in the town of Coronel Bogado. Two of the attackers and a policeman were killed, but the other police officers repulsed the attackers and captured five of them. This attack was followed by a wave of intense police repression throughout the country, with hundreds of leaders of the opposition parties being arrested and tortured. In the town of Coronel Bogado, the captured guerrillas were victims of forced disappearance and extrajudicial execution.

Juan José Rotela, a prominent leader and commander of the M14-V movement. (M. Lachi Archives)

Argentine President Arturo Frondizi. (1958–62) (Public Domain)

The second attempt in 1958 was the so-called 'Bouvier Incident', carried out on 24 October, when around 100 exiles from the Liberal Party in Argentina led by Lieutenant Colonel Eliseo Salinas tried to cross the Paraguay River from Port Bouvier, in the Argentinian province of Formosa, to the city of Villeta in Paraguay. The incursion was aborted because the Argentine Gendarmerie arrested 50 of the insurgents, some of whom were the future leaders of the M14-V.

The origins of the M14-V date back to meetings convened in mid-1958 in Lanús, Buenos Aires, among young Paraguayan exiles who belonged to the Liberal and Febrerista parties. The two initial leaders of the group were the febrerista Arnaldo Valdovinos (1908–91) and the liberal Benjamín Vargas Peña (1910–2003), both veterans of the Chaco War, who were exiled in Buenos Aires after the failure of the 1947 revolution. Both of these leaders criticised the leadership of their political parties for their weakness in confronting the Stroessner regime.

Some of the M14-V armaments captured by the Paraguayan Army. (Instituto de Historia y Museo Militar del MDN)

On 4 May 1959, the faction of the Liberal Party in exile in Buenos Aires led by Benjamín Vargas Peña officially formed the *14 de Mayo* movement, also known as M14-V, and planned a series of attacks on government installations. The name was chosen because Paraguay attained its independence from the Spanish crown through a short and bloodless uprising on 14 May 1811. The M14-V was also joined by the Febreristas led by Arnaldo Valdovinos, who used his contacts with social democratic parties and governments in Latin America (especially in Venezuela) to obtain financial assistance. It was also said that there were contacts with Che Guevara in Cuba to obtain funds. The M14-V founders included several military veterans of the Chaco War and the revolution of 1947, such as Modesto Ramírez, Navy Captain René Speratti, Colonel Alfredo Ramos and Captain Américo Villagra Cano. The famous Paraguayan composer Herminio Giménez also signed the group's founding act.

According to the foundation act, the main purpose of the M14-V was "to fight for the overthrow of the ruling dictatorship in Paraguay and to make possible the advent of an era of freedom for all the people of the nation". A series of meetings were held in order to establish the political objectives, which as well as the overthrow of the dictatorship included the liquidation of its economic, political and social structural system, the total recovery of ill-gotten public and private assets and the punishment of those found guilty of crimes

committed under the rule of the dictatorship. The Constitution of 1940 and subsequent repressive laws would be abolished, and the future government would be ruled by a revolutionary legal statute or the National Constitution of 1870. Members of the Paraguayan Communist Party were not allowed to join the M14-V since only members of democratic parties were accepted, although some foreigners, Argentinians and Uruguayans were permitted. Several Colorado dissidents, members of the MOPOCO (Colorado Popular Movement), also joined the M14-V.

The M14-V was officially presented to the public on 12 June 1959 at an event held in Buenos Aires. The direction of the group was in the hands of a National Revolutionary Board.

As had happened in the 1947 revolution, internal disputes between the Liberals and Febreristas significantly affected the leadership of the M14-V, meaning they could never undertake any major operation against the Stroessner government. Due to such disagreements, the leadership was taken by 26-year-old Juan José Rotela, then president of the Liberal ALON Club in Buenos Aires. Rotela was born on 9 December 1933 near the city of Yegros in Caazapá, Paraguay. Due to political persecution of his family, Rotela went into exile in Buenos Aires when he was only 16 but returned to Paraguay the following year to be drafted for military service in the

Army artillery. Following two years' service, he returned to Buenos Aires.

In the following months, the M14-V leadership worked hard to attract volunteers to the cause, and by September 1959 some 250 Liberals and Febreristas were gathered in Buenos Aires. In order not to alert the Paraguayan government, the volunteers were sent in groups of four or five, either by train or bus, to the provinces of Corrientes and Misiones, both on the border of Paraguay. Once there, they started receiving military training from Chaco War veterans who had joined the M14-V at the farm of Argentine politician Pascual Sarubbi, as well as at the Las Marías ranch which belonged to Víctor Navajas Centeno, some 80km south of the city of Posadas.

There were problems with

M14-V members of the Libertad column during a meeting in Buenos Aires before departing for Paraguay. Seated, from left to right: José Bogarín, Rigoberto Delgado and Rodolfo Serafini. Standing, from left to right: unknown, José Sánchez, Bogado, Garcete, Vierci, Niño Nacimiento Cabrera, Roberto Recalde, unknown, Alfonso, unknown, Clemente Ortega, Blanco, Ramón Lezcano Torres, Garcete, Pedro Alberto Clérici, Teófilo Ramón Sánchez and Raúl Ignacio Castagnino. (Policía Nacional)

the supply of arms and ammunition and they managed to obtain only the following, either from the Argentine Army or on the black market in Buenos Aires: 10 obsolete Lewis machine guns, three .45 pistols, two .38 revolvers, 41 Mauser 7.65mm rifles, 14 submachine guns, three .22 rifles, a single Winchester shotgun, 144 hand grenades, 82 machetes, 137 packages of dynamite, 20 booby-trap bombs, 20 incendiary bombs, 20 tear gas grenades. The following ammunition was acquired: 12,600 7.65mm rounds, 3,548 9mm rounds and 1,260 .45 rounds. They also got hold of 100 detonators, 80 bolts, 60 metres of covered cable, 50 metres of fast fuse and 50 metres of slow fuse for the bombs, and could count on just one old portable radio transmitter, three electric batteries, various tents and some rudimentary medical equipment.

The M14-V initially enjoyed the tolerance of the Argentine civil and military authorities, given that President Stroessner had given Perón political asylum and also because of the Paraguayan dictator's

geopolitical attitude to Brazil. They also obtained the support of the Paraguayan exiles in the provinces of Corrientes and Misiones, as well as several Argentine landowners. However, the Paraguayan government soon became aware of the group's activities and infiltrated police agents into the M14-V; as a consequence, plans for the 'great invasion' were known in advance by the Stroessner regime. Furthermore, a revolutionary cell that was being formed in Asunción for urban guerrilla activities was dismantled by the police. Several members of the M14-V were also unable to keep quiet about the plans, and information was leaked to the press.

The strategy of the M14-V was simple: an assault group and four penetration columns would enter the country simultaneously, aiming to reach the Yvyturusú mountain range to establish a stronghold similar to that of the Cuban revolutionaries in the Sierra Maestra. The main problem was the lack of armaments, meaning that the four columns were poorly equipped, did not carry enough rations,

Left: A Paraguayan Navy petty officer and seaman recruits of the naval base at Encarnación, in the Itapúa region. Right: The Government Delegation building in the city of Encarnación, one of the targets of the M14-V group. (Instituto de Historia y Museo Militar del MDN)

An original armband used by the M14-V fighters. (Policía Nacional)

A Paraguayan Navy motorboat used to patrol the Paraná River. (Armada Paraguaya)

Six former US Coast Guard picket boats were donated to the Paraguayan Navy in 1944 through the Lend-Lease programme and were still in service in the late 1950s. Some were deployed to the Itapúa Naval Base in Encarnación, on the Paraná River, to patrol the border in 1959–60. (Armada Paraguaya)

their training was inadequate and they lacked radio equipment for coordination, all of which seriously affected their chances of success. The revolutionaries had to rely on old radio equipment to transmit, under the code ZPX, but they did not have enough receivers for their troops.

In the early hours of 12 December 1959, under the cover of darkness, one assault group and four rebel columns – in total 250 effectives – crossed the Paraná River to enter Paraguay. The *Libertad* (Liberty) assault group, with 18 members in three boats, was to seize the city of Encarnación. They were led by Juan José Rotela, Arnaldo Clérici and Mario Esteche Notario. Their first main objective was the Paraguayan Coast Guard (*Prefectura Naval*) base, then the base of the Paraguayan Army Frontier Battalion and finally the Government Delegation building. The city contained numerous residents who had agreed to join the operation at the signal of the detonation of a bomb that would be dropped from an Argentine light aircraft. The plan was to establish a permanent beachhead in order to divert the attention of the government's military and police forces so that the penetration columns could silently head towards the Yvyturusú mountain range in the departments of Caazapá and Guairá.

The plan included the capture of several towns in the country, where more volunteers would be incorporated into the ranks of the M14-V, so that upon reaching the Yvyturusú, the group would have a significant number of fighters to later plan an attack on Asunción and the government takeover. The M14-V effectives did not have a standard uniform; most wore civilian clothes, but all had a brown cap with a Paraguayan cockade, and a white armband with the M14-V shield, a black 'M' over two 'V's, one red and one blue.

The Paraná River crossing was made from the summer resort of El Brete, 2km south of the city of Posadas in Misiones, Argentina, but the plan ended in complete failure because the Paraguayan Navy was patrolling the area with motorboats. There was a confrontation between the naval troops and the rebels, who suffered several casualties. The rest of the insurgents from two of the boats were captured. Only one boat, that commanded by Rotela, landed on the Paraguayan shore near Encarnación, but upon learning of the fate of the other two boats, they quickly returned to Posadas. The light airplane to be used was stolen by a Paraguayan pilot at Posadas airport and managed to throw a bomb to alert the M14-V collaborators in Encarnación, but it did not explode so there was no support from within the city. The plane returned to Posadas and the pilot was immediately arrested by the Argentine police. The other M14-V prisoners were transferred to Asunción and then to the Peña Hermosa Military Prison. Most of them managed to escape to Brazil in 1961.

Stroessner had immediately mobilised his cavalry and infantry troops, creating Operational Group Nr. 1 under the command of Brigadier General Hipólito Viveros and Operational Group Nr. 2 under the leadership of Brigadier General Patricio Colmán. They were immediately airlifted to the Itapúa and Caazapá areas by several TAM Douglas C-47s,

Brigadier General Patricio Colmán (left), commander of Operational Group Nr. 2, and Brigadier General Hipólito Viveros (right), commander of Operational Group Nr. 1. (Instituto de Historia y Museo Militar del MDN)

A Military Air Transport (TAM) Douglas C-47 being loaded with troops from Infantry Regiment Nr. 14 to be airlifted to the zone of operations in December 1959. (Fuerza Aérea Paraguaya)

using the landing strips at San Juan Nepomuceno and Encarnación. The area of influence of Operational Group Nr. 1 was the shore of the Paraná River in Itapúa and Alto Paraná, so as to prevent an invasion by more guerrillas from Argentina and the escape of those already in Paraguay. Operational Group Nr. 2 was deployed in the Caazapá region in order to attack and eliminate all guerrillas before they could reach the Yvyturusú mountain range. American COIN experts – both US Army members of the Military Mission in Paraguay and CIA agents – helped the Paraguayan military forces in the field. Cavalry Regiment Nr. 3 troops under the command of Lieutenant Colonel Andrés Rodríguez were sent by air to the Caaguazú and Alto Paraná areas, while Navy gunboats and patrol vessels patrolled the Paraguay and Paraná Rivers. The guerrillas, poorly organised and lightly armed, had no chance of successfully confronting the powerful forces of Stroessner's regime.

It is interesting to note that the government initially referred to the guerrillas as 'subversives', but soon started to call them 'bandits', thus labelling them as armed criminals and never giving them the status of a combat force. This explains why the police were also involved in the repression of these armed movements. The 'bandits' who were captured alive were interrogated by police officers. Once information was obtained from them, usually under torture, their fate was decided: either military prison or immediate execution, normally carried out at night, hidden away in the middle of forests, by troops under the orders of General Patricio Colmán. The Minister of the Interior, Dr Edgar L. Ynsfrán, held several press conferences to issue official statements regarding the capture of the 'bandits' and the number of them 'killed in action'.

The first column, *Mainumby* (Hummingbird in the Guaraní language), with 30 members, was led by former Paraguayan Army Captain Blas Ignacio Talavera and former Lieutenant Servián Brizuela, both Chaco War veterans. They crossed from the town of Puerto Rico in Misiones, Argentina, and landed in Paraguay near the city of Capitán Meza, then reached and took the town of Carlos Antonio López. The group included one woman, Gilberta Verdún de Talavera, the wife of Captain Talavera. The group was attacked and harassed by Paraguayan Army troops, and after four days of marching, half of the guerrillas had deserted. The 13 remaining members of the column continued and reached the area of Ñu Cañy in Caazapá, a

One of the very few pictures of the *Libertad* column still in Argentina, waiting to cross the Paraná River into Paraguay in December 1959. (Policía Nacional)

Paraguayan Air Force North American AT-6C Texans were used to locate and strafe the guerrillas. (Fuerza Aérea Paraguaya)

M14-V fighters in a campsite in a forest in December 1959. All of them are wearing the group's distinctive armbands. (Policía Nacional)

Juan José Rotela (first on the right) and two other M14-V leaders awaiting their fate immediately after being captured by the Paraguayan Army. (Instituto de Historia y Museo Militar del MDN)

made to return to the Paraná River. On 23 December, the remaining M14-V insurgents were intercepted near the river; four were killed in a clash with Army troops, eight more were captured and only one managed to escape to Argentina. One of the detainees tried to escape, but was immediately killed, another died of his injuries. The rest were taken to the town of Capitán Meza, where they were imprisoned.

The second column, *Patria y Libertad* (Homeland and Freedom), comprised 40 members, mainly Febreristas, led by former Paraguayan Army Lieutenants Patricio Ortúzar and Manuel Halley. They crossed the Paraná River from Puerto Iguazú in Argentina with the intention of seizing Puerto Presidente Franco and then attacking Puerto Franco, Puerto Presidente Stroessner and Hernandarias, but one of their boats sank, with the loss of several effectives who drowned. Alerted by the uproar, Paraguayan Army troops opened fire on the survivors, killing their leader, Lieutenant Ortúzar. The other boat reached the Paraguayan shore and took the area of Puerto Embalse (Acaray). They then attacked the town of Hernandarias, capturing the mayor and the Chief of Police in the City Hall for several hours, before deciding to move on to Ytakyry, stealing a truck and a jeep to drive there. However, the town was empty as the Army had evacuated the civilian population. A Paraguayan Air Force North American AT-6C Texan then opened fire on them, so they abandoned their vehicles and moved into the forest in three groups of 10 fighters. They managed to reach the Paraná River on 20 December but were ambushed by a strong Army company led by General Gregorio Morínigo, a Chaco War and revolution of 1947 veteran. Only one member of the group escaped back to Argentina. General Morínigo ignored the order of the Minister of the Interior, Edgar Ynsfrán, not to take prisoners alive, and sent the survivors to Asunción by air on a TAM C-47.

The third column, *Pilar* (a woman's name and also a city in southern Paraguay), led by former Paraguayan Army Captain Modesto Ramírez, a Chaco War veteran and founding member of the M14-V, was supposed to cross the Paraná River from Corrientes in Argentina to seize the city of Pilar, but their only boat was inoperative. Instead, on 15 December, they attempted to capture the Paraguayan Navy boat *Bahia Negra* which was docked

few kilometres from San Juan Nepomuceno. When they learned by radio of the failure of the other columns and saw that the Paraguayan Army was bringing in more troops to the area by air, the decision was

Right: a private of Infantry Regiment Nr. 14 with full gear, holding a Madsen light machine gun. Left: Brigadier General Patricio Colmán giving ammunition to a private before leaving for a patrol in 1960. (Ejército Parguayo)

A Paraguayan Air Force Bell 47G.2 about to land near Army troops deployed to the Caazapá forests in December 1959. (Fuerza Aérea Paraguaya)

The San Juan Nepomuceno (Caazapá) Aerodrome which was used as the Army HQ. Many Army troops were airlifted there to be deployed to the nearby forests to fight the guerrillas. (Fuerza Aérea Paraguaya)

F. Reyes and A. Oviedo and five sailors were wounded during the attack, but all of them survived.

The fourth and final column, *Amambay* (Wild Fern), led by the Febrerista Filemón Valdéz and Gabriel Armoa, intended to seize the city of Pedro Juan Caballero, but all its members were captured and their arms seized by the Brazilian authorities in Ponta Porá.

The first wave of the uprising thus ended in complete failure, resulting in many deaths and nearly 100 prisoners being taken. The Paraguayan authorities also arrested many civilians who were accused of supporting the subversives. Faced with this situation, many M14-V effectives, who were receiving combat training in Argentina for a second attack, cut their ties to the group.

As a consequence of these actions, Alejandro Arce of the Liberal Party and retired Colonel Rafael Franco of the Febrerista Party banned their members from supporting the M14-V group. Regardless of this prohibition, the revolutionaries, especially the younger leaders, wanted to try an invasion one more time. Some of the older founding members of the M14-V attempted to discourage any further military action, even accusing some of the younger leaders of being communists. Nevertheless, a new group of Liberals, Febreristas and even dissident Colorado recruits met in Argentina in Misiones and Resistencia for combat training. Two columns were formed, the 81-man *Libertad* (Liberty), commanded by Juan José Rotela, and the 70-man *Resistencia* (Resistance), led by ex-Navy Captain René Speratti and retired Captain Modesto Ramírez.

A second wave comprising the *Resistencia* and *Libertad* columns met at the campsite in Candelaria, near Corrientes. They were to cross the Paraná River into Paraguayan territory in two large boats on Sunday, 24 April 1960, with the intention of establishing a base in the Yvyturusú mountain range and start a Sierra Maestra-like guerrilla war. On 27 April, both columns marched to Port Piray in Argentina and crossed the river. On 30 April, the *Resistencia* column attacked the town of Port Mayor Otaño in Itapúa, Paraguay, and immediately marched towards the military garrison of Carlos Antonio López. However, they were then strafed by Paraguayan Air Force AT-6Cs and ambushed by Army troops in Guarapay, several of them being killed. The survivors immediately fled the area and headed back towards Argentina, apart from nine insurgents who joined the *Libertad* column. President Stroessner himself airlifted to Carlos Antonio López on a TAM C-47 to learn the very latest on

at the port of Corrientes. Forty insurgents launched an assault on the *Bahia Negra* but were repelled by the crew and were forced to retreat after suffering several casualties, including former Air Force officer Sub-Lieutenant Félix Germán Pérez Núñez. Personnel of the Argentinean Coast Guard captured 29 revolutionaries. The commander of the ship, Navy Captain Ramón Arévalo, NCOs

Paraguayan Army troops of Infantry Regiment Nr. 14 *Cerro Corá* ready for an incursion in the Caazapá forests. (Ejército Paraguayo)

The Paraguayan Army Cessna 180 ambulance which was transferred to the Air Force in the early 1960s. (Fuerza Aérea Paraguaya)

flights departed from the San Juan Nepomuceno airstrip, with AT-6Cs and sometimes Bell 47G.2 helicopters. TAM Douglas C-47s also operated from the airfield, bringing fresh troops to the area and taking wounded officers and soldiers to the capital. Paraguayan Army troops in the area were members of the Infantry Regiment Nr. 14 *Cerro Corá* under the command of General Patricio Colmán. Born in Yegros on 17 March 1913, Colmán fought in the Chaco War. He was trained by the Brazilian Military Mission in Paraguay and took counterinsurgency courses with the US Army in the Panama Canal Zone.

Meanwhile, the *Libertad* column did not see any combat immediately and started marching towards the Yvyturusú range, but in doing so it was located and strafed by Paraguayan Air Force AT-6Cs and pursued by regular Army troops. The guerrillas suffered many casualties, and several of their number were captured.

At the beginning of May, the government had mobilised two operational combat groups: Nr. 1 under the command of General Hipólito Viveros, commander of the Second Department of the General Staff, along the banks of the Paraná River, and Nr. 2 led by General Patricio Colmán, commander of Infantry Regiment Nr. 14. This group had as its chief of staff Colonel Marcial Alborno,

the situation and ordered the torture of the captured guerrillas to obtain information.

Military units were based in the towns of Tavaí, Enramadita, San Juan Nepomuceno, Abay, Tarumá and San Carlos, from where patrols set out to capture as many insurgents as possible. Reconnaissance

The Presidential Cessna 310H ZP-TDR and the Military Air Transport Douglas R4D-1 serial T-35 on an airfield in the conflict zone in the early 1960s. (Fuerza Aérea Paraguaya)

commander of the Military Intelligence. Meanwhile, the Colorado Party began to form an armed civil militia to help the regular forces capture dispersed rebels and deserters. President Stroessner issued orders not to take prisoners. The command post of General Colmán's combat unit was established in the town of Tavaí, 130km east of Caazapá. Military patrols, supported by Air Force AT-6s and Bell 47G.2s, attempted to track down the rebels. Consequently, the guerrillas had to sleep during the day and march at night, but some of them were still found and killed while the rest of them continued on foot towards the Yvyturusú range. General Colmán then moved his headquarters to the city of San Juan Nepomuceno.

From left to right, Paraguayan Army Colonel Marcial Alborno, Lieutenant Apuril and Minister of the Interior Dr Edgar L. Ynsfrán during a meeting at the Army HQ in Tavaí in 1960. (Dr. Edgar Ynsfrán Archives)

On 12 May, the Paraguayan government presented a formal note of protest to its Argentine counterpart over the civil and military authorities in Argentina turning a blind eye to several subversive armed groups that were formed in the country before crossing the border into Paraguay. The note was extremely long, detailing the alleged logistical cooperation, provision of armaments and training of the rebels by the Argentine military. As was expected, the Argentine government denied any involvement in these events and as a consequence, diplomatic relations between the two countries grew strained.

One of the LATN Noorduyn UC-64A Norsemen that was used by the Paraguayan Army as an air ambulance to evacuate casualties to Asunción. (Author's files)

On 20 May, a TAM Douglas C-47 picked up a platoon from Infantry Regiment Nr. 14 in the city of Paraguarí and airlifted it to Tavaí. The platoon was then sent on patrol in the area and several guerrillas were captured and taken to Tavaí. In the afternoon, both General Colmán and Colonel Alborno were taken to Asunción by the same C-47 for a meeting with President Stroessner. After their conference, Colmán and the Minister of the Interior, Edgar L. Ynsfrán, flew to Tavaí in an Air Force Cessna 180 the following day.

On 22 May, troops under the command of Infantry First Lieutenant Juan de Dios Garbett attacked the guerrillas around Guembé-Ybyhati-Ita, Anguá-Ñucañy and Toro Blanco, but the M14-V fighters melted away into the woods. During the following days, even General Colmán led some troops in the area in search of the rebels. The Air Force Cessna 180 remained active performing reconnaissance missions, for which a North American AT-6C was also used. Due to the lack of roads, Army troops had to patrol either on foot or on horseback.

On 25 May, a TAM C-47 airlifted troops from San Juan Nepomuceno to the Enramadita area. On the next day, the Army Command Post was transferred from Tavaí to San Juan Nepomuceno. First Lieutenant Garbett and his troops moved to Enramadita, with those of Major Vega Servián arriving at Capiitindy and Tarumá, and NCO Quinteros with troops of Infantry Regiment Nr. 14 reaching San Carlos. A group of Army sappers was sent to Mbayá. The Army was planning to encircle the guerrillas in the area, and an Air Force AT-6C crewed by Major Adrián Jara and General Colmán flew over the region on 27 May to check the deployment of

Two different groups of M14-V fighters that were captured by the Paraguayan Army. Most of them, once interrogated, were sent to the Military Prison at Peña Hermosa island on the Paraguay River. In the lower picture, one of the guards is posing with the prisoners. (Instituto de Historia y Museo Militar del MDN)

troops. It was then that members of the Colorado militia joined the regular Army troops to take part in patrols. That day, Army troops led by Lieutenant Rivas Sánchez and NCO Quinteros clashed with the guerrillas, who suffered several casualties.

On 31 May, General Hipólito Viveros arrived at Tavaí to exchange information with Colonel Alborno as it was known that some of the rebels had deserted and were trying to return to Argentina. Several hours later, an AT-6C flown by Major Adrian Jara brought the Director of the Technical Affairs of the Paraguayan Police, Dr Antonio Campos Alúm, to interrogate the prisoners.

General Colmán ordered the troops under Majors Eustacio Guillén and Vega Servián to be airlifted to San Juan Nepomuceno immediately. Major Guillén had been trained in counterinsurgency tactics and armament at the School of the Americas (SOA) at USARCARIB (United States Army Caribbean) in the Panama Canal Zone in 1954 and 1956.

On 1 June, Army troops led by Major Vega Servián fought the guerrillas near the town of Santo Tomé, 40km north of Tavaí. During a half-hour firefight, three members of the M14-V were killed, along with one of the Army troops, a private. A further two M14-V fighters were captured. Air strips were then built at Capiitindy and Cecina so that small Cessnas and Beechcrafts could land. On the next day, a Noorduyn Norseman which belonged to LATN landed in San Juan Nepomuceno in order to transport the body of the dead private to Asunción.

There were several further clashes in the area between the rebels and Army troops, as a consequence of which the largest group of guerrillas was disbanded, leaving most of their weapons and ammunition in the woods. Throughout May, the M14-V suffered numerous desertions that diminished its operational force and stock of weapons. Most of the deserters tried to reach Argentina but were chased by Army troops; some made it to safety but most of them were killed. A small group of 10 rebels, still led by Rotela, decided to continue towards the Yvyturusú region. On 1 June, some of the disbanded guerrillas were attacked by Army forces; almost all of them were killed, only one of them finally reaching the banks of the Paraná River and crossing to safety in Argentina. Army troops and the Colorado militia also located and killed M14-V members in the woods near the towns of Santa María, Capitán Meza, Carlos A. López and Paranambú.

Rotela and his few remaining fighters continued their march on 5 June, reaching the area around Guairá, keeping to the forests to avoid detection. However, they all then decided to return to Argentina, with the help of indigenous people who knew the area well and set off on foot to the east. They were in low spirits, in poor physical condition or ill, completely

The Minister of Public Works, Brigadier General Marcial Samaniego, and Minister of Defence, Major General Leodegar Cabello, arriving at the Army HQ in San Juan Nepomuceno in 1960 on a Military Air Transport Douglas C-47. (Fuerza Aérea Paraguaya)

A Military Air Transport Consolidated Vultee PBY-5A Catalina and a pair of Douglas C-47s at Alejo García Airport in Puerto Presidente Stroessner in 1960. (Fuerza Aérea Paraguaya)

deprived of food and with very few weapons and little ammunition.

On 8 June, the Paraguayan Army Chief of Staff, Major General Leodegar Cabello, sent a note to the Chief of the US Army Mission in Paraguay, Brigadier General Beverly D. Jones, to inform him that three senior officers – Brigadier General Hipólito Viveros, Colonel Marcial Alborno and Major Carlos Jorge Fretes Dávalos – had been selected by the Paraguayan government to attend a conference of Latin American military chiefs in the Panama Canal Zone, to be held between 8 and 12 August of that year. The theme was the fight against subversive groups throughout the region.

M14-V guerrillas at a campsite in the Caazapá forests. (Policía Nacional)

On 9 June, the government deployed Cavalry Regiment Nr. 1 to Puerto Presidente Stroessner, three TAM Douglas C-47s and a LATN PBY-5A Catalina used to transport the troops. Several days later, on the 16th, an Army patrol led by Navy Lieutenant Amadeo Rodriguez Gaona captured four rebels in the Abay area. Both the guerrillas and the Army troops employed aborigine guides in the woods, members of the Mbyá nation who lived in the region.

On 22 June, Rotela and his group exchanged fire with Army personnel, suffering several casualties. Then on 4 July, a further clash further decimated the ranks of the rebels in the Ñacunday area, with only Rotela and four members surviving of the original 80 effectives who had entered the country at the end of April. The next day, an urgent meeting was held between the military commander chief of staff and the Minister of the Interior in the city of Puerto Presidente Stroessner in Alto Paraná in order to plan the hunting down and killing of Rotela and all his surviving rebels as soon as possible. At that time, a Paraguayan Army patrol of 15 men led by Lieutenant Garbett were chasing Rotela's group. On 8 July, the group

was surrounded at Paranambú, and after a brief exchange of fire they were killed on the banks of the Paraná River by patrols from Infantry Battalion Nr. 1 and Cavalry Regiment Nr.1. Their corpses were thrown into the Paraná River. Only Rotela was captured alive, at Port Ordóñez, and he was transferred by plane on 10 July, under the custody of Majors Rodríguez and Samaniego, to the command post of General Colmán at the Tapytá ranch between the towns of San Juan Nepomuceno and Tavaí in Caazapá. Rotela was subjected to a lengthy police interrogation, including torture, and was executed on 12 July on the orders of General Colmán. During a press conference given by the Ministry of the Interior, it was stated that all the guerrillas were killed in combat, although most of them were actually captured by the Army and later executed. The press and the general public were told that Rotela 'was killed in combat' in the vicinity of the town of Domingo Martínez de Irala, close to the Paraná River.

On 11 October 1960, eight members of the M14-V group, under the command of Carlino Colinas, left the Pareja-í camp in Misiones, Argentina, with the intention of helping and providing

Capitán PAM Ángel Souto H. Tcnel. DEM Epifanio Cardozo Tcnel. DEM René Zotti Mayor PAM Bernardo Gamarra

Mayor DEM Adrián Jara Mayor PAM Pedro A. Valenzuela Mayor PAM Blas Marín C. Mayor PAM Luis A. González R.

Paraguayan Air Force pilots who flew AT-6Cs, Bell 47G.2s, Douglas C-47s, PBY-5A Catalinas, Beechcraft A35 Bonanzas and Cessna 180s to the zone of operations in 1959–60. (Fuerza Aérea Paraguaya)

Brazilian President Jânio da Silva Quadros. (Public Domain)

logistical support to those guerrillas from the *Libertad* column who had not yet been captured or killed. They were unaware that all of their number had been arrested and executed three months earlier. They disembarked in Puerto Palma, near the city of Hernandarias, intending to walk all the way to the town of Yhú and then reach the Yvyturusú mountain range. An aborigine captured by the group, who later escaped, alerted the authorities and once again, Army troops were deployed in the area. Some 70km before reaching Yhú, the guerrillas were attacked by the troops and were forced to head north.

Over a period of two months, the government troops chased the guerrillas, with several Air Force Beechcraft 35 Bonanzas also being used to try to locate them. On 17 November, the rebels captured and killed two members of the Colorado militia who had been taking food to the Army troops in the area. The next clash came on 28 November, when an Army officer of Cavalry Regiment Nr. 1 *Valois Rivarola*, Lieutenant Moisés Galeano, and Private Emiliano López Irala were killed by the guerrillas. Exhausted and malnourished, the insurgents decided to go to Brazil on 18 December, attempting to reach the campsite of exiled members of the M14-V led by Filemón Valdéz, near the city of Paranhos.

The presence of these guerrillas was not welcomed in Brazil, and municipal officials of Paraguayan descent informed Paraguayan troops in the border town of Ypejhú of their movements. It was planned to deceive the guerrillas by telling them that they would be taken to a Brazilian Army base for their protection. A truck picked them up on the night of 24 December, and once all were on board, it headed towards the border. Once there, immediately after the group got off the truck, they were shot by a squad of Paraguayan Army troops in what became known as the 'Christmas Eve massacre'. Only two rebels survived: Antonio Arce, who pretended to be dead, and Remigio Giménez, who ran off into the forest. A couple of months later, Brazilian president Jânio Quadros presented a formal protest to Paraguay for the violation of Brazil's sovereignty and then granted political asylum to the two guerrillas who had escaped alive.

After the failed attempts described above, the last action carried out by the M14-V was on 21 December 1960. Sixty men under the command of former Major Juan Bartolomé Araujo were prepared to carry out an incursion across the Paraguay River towards the port of Itá Enramada. However, this raid was aborted due to the arrest, the

From left to right, Colonel DEM Marcial Alborno, Minister of the Interior Dr Edgar L. Ynsfrán and Brigadier General Patricio Colmán discussing plans to deal with the rebels at the Army Command Post in the Tapytá ranch in 1960. (Dr Ynsfrán Archives)

day before, of logistical support groups in Paraguay led by Cándido Rotela and former Lieutenant Mazó. After this episode, the M14-V ceased to function as an armed movement against Stroessner.

Some 120 guerrillas who had been captured during the clashes in 1959 and 1960 were initially held in inhumane conditions at the prison of the Police Security Guard Battalion in Asunción. They were savagely tortured and forced to work breaking stones in the Tacumbú quarry. In mid-1960, 49 of the detainees were sent to the military prison of Peña Hermosa, an island located in the middle of the Paraguay River, 500km north of Asunción. Living conditions

there were much better, and when Jânio Quadros, who opposed the regime of Stroessner, was elected President of Brazil, the detainees in Peña Hermosa began to plan a large-scale escape so that they could live in exile over the border in Brazil. The first group of five prisoners managed to leave the island on 23 March 1961 and walked 190km to freedom in the Brazilian state of Matto Grosso. Then on 27 April, a mass mutiny in Peña Hermosa resulted in the rest of the detainees escaping. Once near the Brazilian border, they were fired upon by troops of the Paraguayan Army, but almost all of them, even those who were wounded, were able to cross the frontier to safety. Only one member of the group was arrested and sent back to Asunción. All the others received political asylum in Brazil, with even President Quadros visiting them in São Paulo.

The fate of the M14-V had been sealed because the group had neither the official support of the authorities of the Liberal and Febrerista parties nor of the common people in Paraguay. Barely armed, with poor logistics, severe leadership problems, without clear objectives and the way to achieve them, and being profoundly naïve regarding the supposed support they would receive from the general population, they went into a suicidal combat against a very powerful and organised military force. Of the 250 effectives who participated in the actions, 120 were captured and sent to prison, but 48 of these escaped to Brazil in 1961. Some 54 guerrillas were either killed in combat or after being captured, and 38 were listed as missing in action. The rest of the group, numbering 38 insurgents, returned to Argentina.

4

THE FULNA

The resounding failure of the M14-V did not discourage the Paraguayan communist leaders from forming another guerrilla group, which they called FULNA (*Frente Unido de Liberación Nacional*, United Front for National Liberation), a Marxist-Leninist organisation whose members were mainly communists but also included some Febreristas. They were openly supported by the Paraguayan Communist Party (*Partido Comunista Paraguayo*, PCP). FULNA was born at a time when the M14-V was still operating in the forests of Paraguay, and they were even rivals in some aspects. In fact, the hasty decision to launch a communist guerrilla movement came partly out of fear of remaining in the shadows of the bourgeois interests of the M14-V group.

In February 1959, while the FULNA was still being created in Buenos Aires, similar work was also being done in the interior of Paraguay. In the Cordillera, Tebicuary-mí and Paraguarí areas, intense propaganda aimed at the peasants began, with the slogan of the 'general uprising of the people'. The so-called 'Village' was organised as the support body for the enrolment of volunteers for the Mariscal López column. In addition to this, other fronts were also being formed, such as the Yvytyrusú in Guairá, San Pedro and in the south of the country. The *Ytororó* column (a Guaraní language word meaning waterfall) was being structured politically and militarily in the north of Argentina, with its command, different attack sections and auxiliary organs, including a propaganda arm, organised in cells. Members of the column went through stages of military training and political indoctrination.

The success of the Cuban Revolution inspired both the FULNA and M14-V guerrilla groups in Paraguay, but Paraguay was not Cuba and these groups failed miserably. Bolivia was not Cuba either, and Che Guevara was captured and executed there in 1967. (Public Domain)

The general secretary of the Paraguayan Communist Party, Oscar Adalberto Creydt (left), and the then Chilean socialist senator Dr Salvador Allende Gossens (right). (Public Domain)

Prominent leaders of the Paraguayan Communist Party in exile in Buenos Aires. From left to right: Mrs Dora Frei de Barthe, Agustín Barboza, Obdulio Barthe, Oscar Creydt and José Asunción Flores. (Arq. Jorge Rubiani Archives)

of the PCP. During the revolution of 1947, he stayed in Asunción underground, but after the defeat of the uprising he went into exile to Buenos Aires. In 1952, he visited the Soviet Union, and the following year was appointed as General Secretary of the PCP. After the 1958 general strike in Paraguay, he supported the armed fight against the Stroessner regime. On 27 August 1959, he called on the peasants and workers to be prepared for an armed struggle. He also harshly criticised the M14-V movement for not following the Cuban model.

The official launch of the FULNA took place on 16 September 1959 in the auditorium of the University of the Republic in Montevideo, Uruguay. The main speaker at the occasion was the Chilean senator Salvador Allende, who was later President of Chile. One of the FULNA leaders, Zaldívar Villagra, also gave a speech, rejecting any agreement with the dictatorship.

On 29 December of that year, the three main leaders of the PCP – Oscar Creydt, Obdulio Barthe and Augusto Cañete – released a document entitled 'Transforming the armed movement into a democratic revolution of the people. It is the only way to win', which expedited preparations for the armed struggle. Meanwhile, the Stroessner government and the CIA prepared a list of 40 Paraguayan citizens who were members of the Liberal, Febrerista and Communist parties, as well as several dissidents from the Colorado Party, who had been trained in Cuba since 1960.

By the beginning of 1960, the PCP had already established another FULNA guerrilla column, called *Mariscal López* (Marshal Francisco Solano López was the President of Paraguay and the Commander-in-Chief of the Army during the Triple Alliance War of 1864–70 against Brazil, Argentina and Uruguay), on Kaundy Hill, near the city of Piribebuy. The commanders of this column were Wilfrido Álvarez, from the PCP's Campesino Front, and Arturo López, alias Agapito Valiente. The second in command was Celso Ávalos Ocampos and the third Romilio López. The first command was a military one, while the other two were purely political.

During the first three months of 1960, the *Mariscal López* column, in compliance with a tactical training and logistics plan, started stealing armaments from the police and armed forces in

The FULNA was formed as a hasty reaction to the euphoria created by the success of the Cuban Revolution. It was formally created in February 1959 and was headed by former Lieutenant Colonels Fabián Zaldívar Villagra and Lorenzo Arrúa, who had been commanders of the Army Infantry Regiment Nr. 2 and later leaders of the revolutionaries in the civil war of 1947.

Just as in Cuba the great general strike of 1958 against the Batista regime did not obtain the expected results and Fidel Castro decided to turn to an armed struggle, a general strike in Paraguay in August 1958 was also defeated. The Paraguayan Communist Party drew a simplistic conclusion: it would follow the Cuban guerrilla model.

The General Secretary of the PCP between 1953 and 1965 was Oscar Adalberto Creydt. Born in San Miguel, Paraguay, on 6 November 1907, the grandson of a German immigrant, he studied law at the National University and was one of the founding members

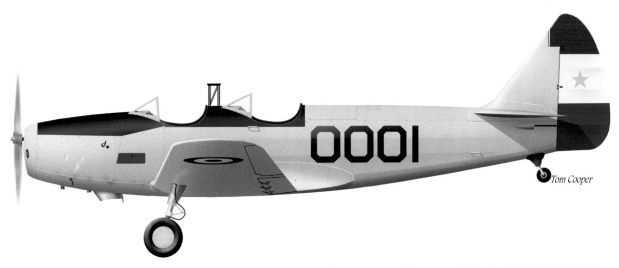

Finished in the US-made colour similar to the British-made Specification DTD772 high-speed silver finish, this Fairchild PT-19A was acquired through the Lend-Lease Program of 1942–1943. Like the entire fleet, it received the serial 0001, applied in the large 'Amarillo USAF' fonts on the rear fuselage, and served as a primary trainer. (Artwork by Tom Cooper)

Between 1956 and 1959, Paraguay acquired 14 Galeão PT-3FG primary trainers from Brazil: these were Fairchild PT-19As manufactured under licence in Brazil. Easily recognisable as Brazilian-made examples, they all had their wings painted in orange overall. As customary with the Paraguayan Air Arm – where they were known as 'T-19s' (as in Brazil) – they received large, black, four-digit serials applied in the Amarillo USAF font on the rear fuselage. (Artwork by Tom Cooper)

A total of 10 Vultee BT-13As were donated to Paraguay through the Lend-Lease Program in 1942–1943, while two additional examples were purchased from Argentina in 1947. Three additional BT-13s were acquired form the Argentine Naval Aviation in 1960. In the Paraguayan Air Arm, they served in their original overall livery similar to the high-speed silver, and wore the usual large, black, four-digit serials on the rear fuselage. (Artwork by Tom Cooper)

In 1943, the Paraguayan Air Arm received the first three North American AT-6C Texan basic trainers and light strikers through the Lend-Lease Program. All three saw action during the revolution of 1947, and even more so during COIN operations of 1959–1965, when they were the only armed aircraft in Paraguayan service. At that time, all were in bare metal overall finish, and wore the usual large, black, four-digit serials on the rear fuselage. (Artwork by Tom Cooper)

In addition to 0101, illustrated above, the other two Paraguayan AT-6Cs operational as of 1959–1965 wore serials 0103 and 0105. For their easier identification, during the 1960s they received a red band around the engine cowling (replaced by red fuselage bands in the 1970s). As well as one 7.62mm machine gun installed internally in front of the right side of the cockpit, they frequently had another Browning M2 in the rear cockpit, and could be armed with up to four US-made 100lbs (50kg) AN-M30 general-purpose bombs on underwing hardpoints. (Artwork by Tom Cooper)

In 1955 Paraguay purchased two Bell 47G-2 light helicopters directly from the factory. Painted in yellow overall, they were deployed intensively during the COIN operations of 1959–1965, when one wore the serial H-003, as illustrated here. Eight additional OH-13Hs were donated by the USA within the MAP to the Paraguayan Air Arm in 1972, and four to the Naval Aviation. (Artwork by Luca Canossa)

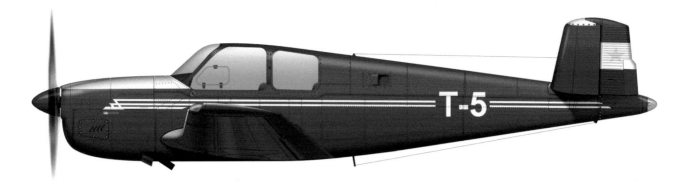

In 1949 the Paraguayan Air Arm acquired a brand-new Beechcraft A.35 Bonanza basic trainer in the USA. Painted in red overall, this received the serial T-5. Six additional Bonanzas were acquired between 1949 and 1967. (Artwork by Anderson Subtil)

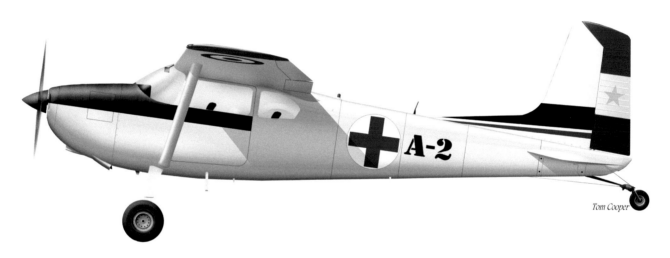

In 1957, the Health Corps of the Paraguayan Army acquired a single Cessna 180A – originally wearing the registration ZP-TBM – from the Paraguayan Ministry of Health and Welfare. Painted in white overall, the aircraft was used by the Army as a flying ambulance until 1962, when it was transferred to the Paraguayan Air Arm, where it received the serial T-19. (Artwork by Tom Cooper)

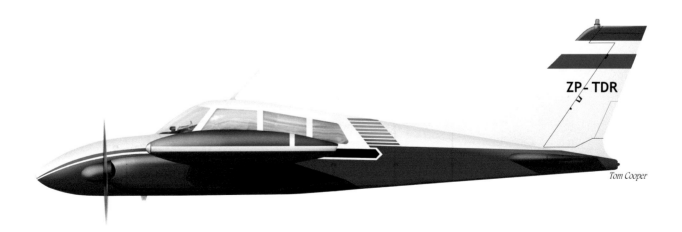

This Cessna 310H (registration ZP-TDR) was acquired in 1963 and operated by pilots of the Paraguayan Air Arm for the Presidency of the Republic. It saw intensive deployment during COIN operations and was withdrawn from service only in 1989. (Artwork by Tom Cooper)

Paraguayan Naval Aviation Vultee BT-13A serial NAVAL 110. Three BT-13s were donated by the Argentine Naval Aviation to its Paraguayan counterpart in 1960. They were in service until the late 1960s. (Artwork by Luca Canossa)

In 1958, the two UC-45Fs were reinforced through the acquisition of a single Beechcraft AT-11, operated by the Paraguayan Air Arm until 1963. This aircraft was also left in bare metal overall, but had its cabin painted in white and received a red cheat line. Following a minor accident, the front transparency was completely removed and replaced with a solid nose. Wearing the serial T-3, the Paraguayan AT-11 was home-based at Ñu-Guazú AFB, and primarily deployed as a light transport. (Artwork by Tom Cooper)

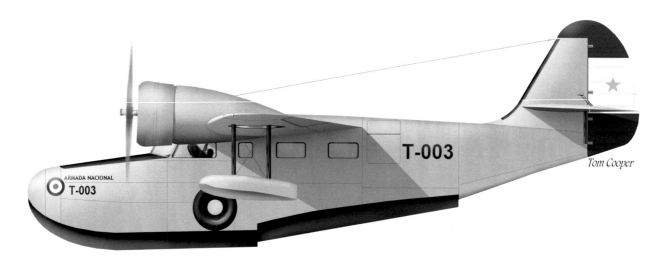

The Paraguayan Naval Aviation acquired three Grumman JRF-5 Goose amphibians in 1958. With one lost during the ferry flight, only two actually reached Paraguay, including the example illustrated here, serial T-003. All were painted in a livery reminiscent of the high-speed silver finish from Great Britain, and had their undersides painted in black. (Artwork by Tom Cooper)

The sole de Havilland DH.104 Dove was donated to the Paraguayan Air Arm in 1962 and used exclusively as a presidential aircraft. The light grey colour applied overall at first was eventually removed and replaced with bare metal overall. The aircraft retained its red cheatline and was painted in white along the upper side of the cabin and on the fin until the end of its service life in 1972. The nose and the upper half of the engine cowlings were always painted in matt black, as was the serial T-39, applied on the rear fuselage. (Artwork by Tom Cooper)

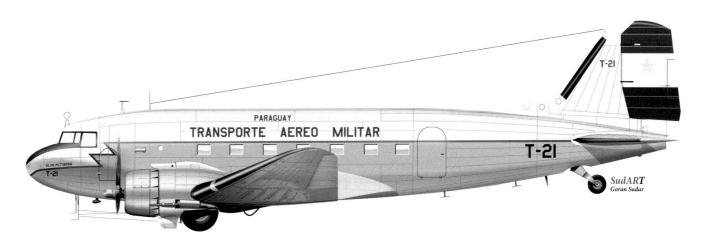

In 1953, the Military Air Transport (TAM) of the Paraguayan Air Arm acquired its first Douglas DC-3A-G202A, serialled T-21, purchased in the USA. As well as being used as a troop-transport during COIN operations, it served as a TAM-operated airliner until damaged beyond repair in a heavy storm of 1963, and withdrawn from service. (Artwork by Goran Sudar)

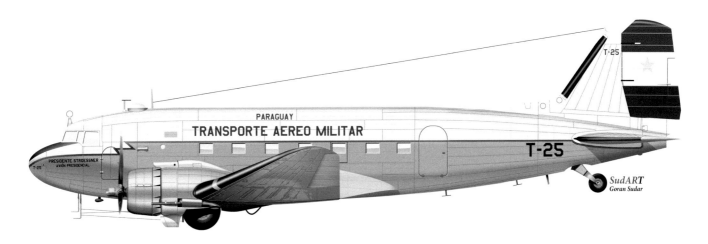

In 1955, the TAM acquired its third 'Dakota': a Douglas DC-3A-269B, serial number T-25. As well as serving as an airliner operated by the TAM, it was also used as the presidential aircraft. Serial number T-25 was completely destroyed in a fire that erupted while it was refuelled at Encarnación airstrip, in 1964, during preparations for a scheduled flight. (Artwork by Goran Sudar)

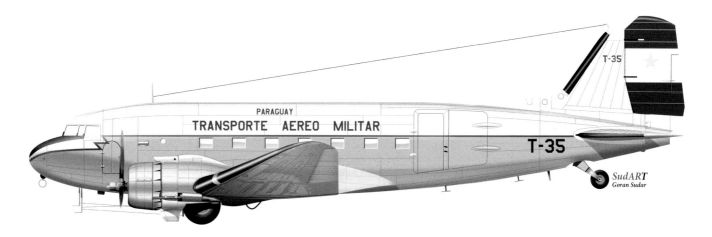

Also in 1955, the Paraguayan Air Arm acquired this Douglas R4D-1. Serialled T-35, the aircraft served with the TAM for nearly three decades: from 1970 until 1974, it was operated by the Líneas Aéreas Paraguayas (LAP) as ZP-CCG, and in 1980, it was re-serialled as FAP 2007. This R4D was eventually withdrawn from service only in 1982. (Artwork by Goran Sudar)

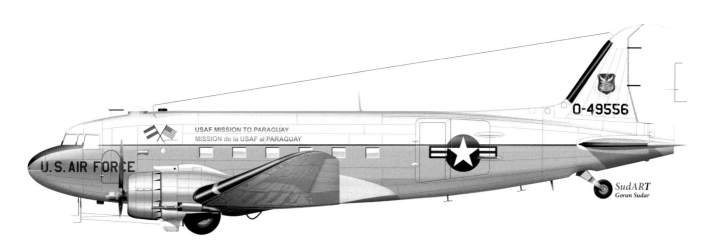

The United States Air Force Mission in Paraguay was equipped with this Douglas C-47 (serial 0-49556) from 1955 until 1956, from 1961 until 1963, and from 1967 until 1968. Primarily used as a transport by the Americans, it also served to provide instruction to TAM pilots and maintenance personnel. (Artwork by Goran Sudar)

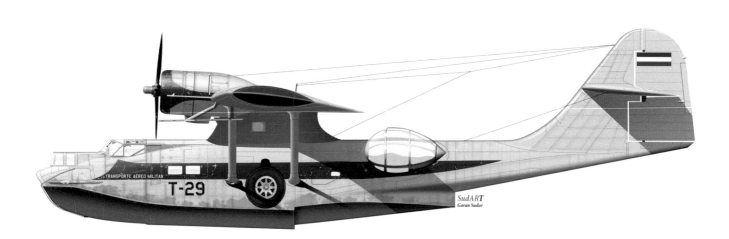

The TAM of the Paraguayan Air Arm acquired three Consolidated Vultee PBY-5A Catalina amphibians from the USA in 1955. One of them was destroyed during a test-flight before delivery, and only two reached Paraguay. While the other example – serial T-31 – was destroyed in an accident on the Paraguay River in 1957, the other – serial T-29 – saw a long and distinguished career. When operated for civilian purposes by the TAM it wore the civilian registration ZP-CBA. In 1955, it rescued the former Argentine president Juan Perón from Buenos Aires. Completely overhauled in 1988, it was re-serialled FAP 2002, until being sold back to the USA in 1991. (Artwork by Goran Sudar)

In the 1970s, the Brazilian Air Force donated 17 North American T-6Gs (left) and 12 (armed)
T-6Ds to Paraguay. (Via José de Alvarenga & João Paulo Zeitun Moralez)

A Grumman JRF-6B Goose of the Paraguayan Naval Aviation, seen on the Paraguya
River, in Bahia Negra (Chaco), in the 1960s. (Luis Rodriguez Scorza)

Shown wearing their classic green fatigues, these two photographs shown the Paraguayan Army's infantry during a parade
in Asunción in the early 1970s. The platoon on the left are armed with M1 Garand rifles (with one NCO carrying an M3 'Grease
Gun' SMG), and those in the image to the right with the M20 'Super-Bazooka' anti-tank rocket launcher. (Ejército Paraguayo)

COIN Operations in Paraguay

THE M14-V PLAN

- First Phase
- Second Phase
- Third Phase

Legend
- Army Military Regions in 1950s
- Cities
- Ybuturuzú Montain Range
- FULNA infiltration
- Airlifted Troops

Chaco Western Region

Mariscal Estigarribia
Chaco Military Region HQ

Argentina

Paraguay

Brazil

Apa River

Concepción

Pedro Juan Caballero

Amambay Column

Eastern Region

Paraguay River

Asunción (Capital)

Villarrica

Abay

Charará

San Juan Nepomuceno

Tapytá Ranch

Tavai

Cap. Meza

San Juan Bautista

Pilar

Paraná River

Pto. Pte. Stroessner

Patria y Libertad Column

Mayor Otaño

Puerto San José

Ytororó Column FULNA

Encarnación

Mainumby Column

Libertad Assault Group

Pilar Column

Army Operational Group Nr. 1

Army Operational Group Nr. 2

In 1954, Genearl Alfredo Stroessner ousted Federico Chaves from the presidency of Paraguay, beginning the longest-lasting Latin American dictatorship. A few years later, the exiled opposition in Argentina realised that the only way to overthrow Stroessner was through armed struggle. The Liberal- and Febrerista Parties allied to form the 'Movimiento 14 de Mayo' (M-14V), while members of the Paraguayan Communist Party created the Frente Unido de Liberación Nacional (FULNA). With inadequate training, equipped with obsolete weapons and poor logistics, the rebels that entered Paraguay gained little support and underestimated the capacity of the Paraguayan Army, which mobilised its troops by air, quickly overcoming them. The vast majority of the insurgents ended up killed in combat, or imprisoned by Army troops and murdered after torture. The remnants hid in the mountains of the Cordillera del Ybyturuzú until they were captured and killed in mid-1965.

THE M14-V FINAL ATTEMPT

- M-14-V Columns
- Paraguayan Army
- Airlifted Army Troops

Puerto Pte. Stroessner

Alto Paraná

Puerto Paranambú

Mayor Otaño

Resistencia Column

Puerto Piray (Argentina)

Libertad Column

Carlos Antonio Lópes

Guarapay

Santo Tomé

Tavai

San Juan Nepomuceno

Abay

Guairá

Caazapá

Itapúa

FULNA ATTEMPT

- FULNA Columns
- Paraguayan Army
- Airlifted Troops

Two other planned columns did not materialize, Rodríguez do Francia in 1963 in Brazil and Mariscal Estigarribia in 1964 in Paraguay;

Alto Paraná

Puerto/Pte. Stroessner

Puerto Ordoñez

Puerto Paranambú

Mayor Otaño

Puerto San José

Capitán Meza

Caaguazú

Tavai

Pelanca

Coronel Bogado

Encarnación

Itapúa

Caazapá

Santo Tomé

Abay

Cerro Corá

San Juan Nepomuceno

Guairá

Eusebio Ayala

Mcal. López Column

Kamdy Hill

Piribebuy

Central

Asunción

FULNA

(Map by Anderson Subtil)

Three FULNA guerrilla leaders, from left to right, Arturo López, alias Agapito Valiente, Antonio Alonso Ramírez and the former Air Force Lieutenant Adolfo Ávalos Carísimo. (Policía Nacional)

The Minister of the Interior, Dr Edgar L. Ynsfrán (in civilian clothes), meeting high-ranking Army officers at Asunción International Airport in 1960. (Dr Ynsfrán Archives)

attention of the police and the Army from the arrival of the *Ytororó* column. They suddenly burst into a meeting of the local authorities, who had earlier met with the chief of police of the government delegation. Arturo López led the action from a safe distance, unseen by anyone. The guerrillas seized radio equipment and quickly left the city for the nearby forest. Security forces which arrived half an hour later were unable to pursue them. This FULNA raid took the government by surprise, and as a consequence, a huge programme repression was established in the area. Around 300 peasants from the towns of Barrero Grande, Isla Pucú, Caraguatay and Itacurubí were arrested and gathered at the telegraph and telephone office in Barrero Grande. They were later sent to the Police Investigation Department, the Police Security Guard and the Police Office for Technical Affairs in Asunción, where they were interrogated and tortured. Most of them were then set free, but those of whom the authorities remained suspicious were sent to a military prison in Ingavi, Chaco. Despite these reprisals, none of the guerrilla members who participated in the Barrero Grande raid were found.

The FULNA incursions from Argentina started on 13 June 1960, involving 54 members of the *Ytororó* column (51 men and three women), led by former Air Force Lieutenant Adolfo Ávalos Carísimo. Leaving their camp near Corrientes in Argentina and crossing the Paraná River north of San Rafael, Misiones, two days later, like the M14-V group they were badly organised and poorly armed, having to fight against very well-equipped and organised forces of the Paraguayan Army. Indeed, the FULNA column made the same mistakes as had the M14-V group, disembarking in the same place, Puerto San José, and following the same route as the other guerrillas had traversed – San Rafael–Pelanca–Abay–Tavaí – only six weeks before. However, the FULNA's guerrilla strategy was different from that of the M14-V, preferring the prolonged war that had brought victory to the Chinese communists led by Mao Zedong in 1949. FULNA fighters were not supposed to openly oppose government forces, but rather support peasant cells in order to prepare a great popular uprising against the Stroessner regime.

Cynically, the PCP's Creydt ordered the *Ytororó* column to go to the same area as Rotela's M14-V group, under the excuse of offering

Paraguay, as obtaining weapons was vital for its plans. Arturo López had already begun operating as early as 1958 in the city of Piribebuy during a workers' strike. He was apprehended by Fidencio Pérez, a Colorado leader who tortured and publicly humiliated him in the main square of Piribebuy. Immediately after these events, López went into hiding, from which he would not emerge until his death.

On 4 May 1960, Antoliano Cardozo, an organiser of the FULNA guerrilla bases around Santa Catalina in Caazapá, was arrested by the urban guard (Colorado militia) and sent to the armed forces base in Charará, where he was tortured by Police Commissioners Taponier and Hellman.

On 10 May, The Sparrow Brigade (*Brigada Los Gorriones*), made up of high school and university students, began to distribute FULNA brochures to the population in Asunción and painted walls with proclamations supporting the movement. The police reacted quickly by arresting those students they learned were involved.

On the night of 24 May, 13 members of the *Mariscal López* column, led by Celso Ávalos Ocampos, attacked the town of Barrero Grande (now the city of Eusebio Ayala) in an attempt to divert the

The Paraguayan police Security Guard was an elite group of the national police that saw action against the guerrillas in 1959 and 1960. (Milda Rivarola Archives)

Paraguay's Minister of the Interior, Dr Edgar L. Ynsfrán (fifth from the right), posing with various civilian and military authorities next to a TAM C-47 at Asunción International Airport in 1960 before travelling to the theatre of operations in Caazapá. (Dr. Ynsfrán Archives)

them support. However, the Army had already decimated the *Libertad* column and was well aware of the *Ytororó* invasion. The FULNA guerrillas thus walked straight into the lion's den. The only logistics support they received was given by some PCP guerrillas who had reached the Yvyturusú mountain range in December 1959, led by Antonio Alonso Ramírez. Ramírez had been captured by the Army in May 1960 and sent to the Army Command Post in Charará, where he was interrogated by the Minister of the Interior, Edgar L. Ynsfrán. He was later tortured and killed under General Colmán's orders in front of local peasants, to serve as an example of what would happen to them if they helped the rebels. Several students were also arrested in Asunción during May that year for distributing leaflets containing FULNA proclamations.

The regime's response to the FULNA incursion was even more severe than it had been against the M14-V guerrillas, orders being issued to exterminate all of them, with no prisoners to be taken. Just after crossing the river, the FULNA rebels set off on foot towards Pelanca and Abay. On 15 June, Army Lieutenant Berino was given command of a platoon in a clandestine mission to kidnap

Presidential visits were made to the zone of the Army operations. The picture on the left shows President Stroessner in military uniform about to leave for the Army Command Post in San Juan Nepomuceno in December 1959. On the right, Stroessner is in civilian clothes in an Army jeep at the Army Command Post in Ñu-Cañy on 30 June 1960. (Fuerza Aérea Paraguaya)

a FULNA member in Argentina and force him, under torture, to reveal the FULNA plans. The Argentine press roundly denounced this violation of its territory by Paraguayan troops, and relations between the governments of Stroessner in Paraguay and Frondizi in Argentina reached a critical point. Paraguay, for its part, denounced Argentina for its provision of logistical support, training and weapons for the guerrillas.

The first clashes took place on 19 June, only four days after the FULNA rebels entered the country. On 28 June, Infantry Regiment Nr. 14 troops, led by General Colmán, mounted a surprise attack on the guerrilla camp in Ñu Cañy, 15km south of the town of Tavaí, Caazapá. The guerrillas suffered heavy casualties, the few survivors dispersing in small groups into the forests, but even they were soon captured, interrogated, tortured and then murdered. After the confrontation, Army troops also captured a large quantity of materiel, including a medical kit, typewriter, 300 communist brochures, nursing and combat manuals, radio receivers, food supplies, rifles, ammunition and hand grenades. Some 30 peasants who had provided food aid to the guerrillas were also captured and killed by Infantry Regiment Nr. 14 troops under Major Daniel Larrosa.

Early on the morning of 30 June, President Stroessner and the commanders of major military units arrived on a TAM C-47 at the command post at Ñu-Cañy, where they were informed of the latest confrontation with the insurgents. After the meeting, the command post was moved to the Tapytá ranch. From there, Army troops, aided by a number of Colorado militiamen, captured 10 FULNA fighters, who were taken to the ranch command post. Once there, they were interrogated by the police, tortured and murdered. Urgent airlifts of military chiefs and officers were carried out by Beechcraft and Cessna aircraft of the Air Force, especially if the air strips at the sites were short. Only when the Commander-in-Chief, Stroessner, and troops were deployed were TAM Douglas C-47s used to locations where there were longer runways, such as San Juan Nepomuceno, Tavaí, Encarnación or Puerto Presidente Stroessner.

On 2 July, a Paraguayan Army patrol captured seven members of the *Ytororó* column, including two women, between the towns of San Gabriel and Toro Blanco. The captured guerrillas suffered the same fate as their comrades. Meanwhile, the command of Cavalry Regiment Nr. 1, whose base was in the city of Puerto Presidente Stroessner, was ordered to send patrols along the shore of the Paraná River in order to intercept and capture all the guerrillas who tried to return to Argentina.

Possible tactical support for the last survivors of the *Ytororó* column was thwarted by the arrest in Itapé, in the Department of Guairá, of 'Commander Gill', Antonio Alonso Ramírez, another PCP leader. Despite his torture, the police did not obtain any information from 'Gill', but the prisoner was still put to death. On 4

Some of the FULNA insurgents who were captured by the Paraguayan Army. Very few of them survived to tell the tale. (Policía Nacional)

July, a FULNA cell composed of six guerrillas under the command of Ávalos Ocampos was heading towards Pirayú when it was surrounded by Army troops led by Lieutenant Buzarquis in the Yjeré area, near the city of Piribebuy. Several of the insurgents were able to escape, but those who were wounded were captured. On the 13th, Juan Bautista Rondelli, a member of the Central Committee of the Paraguayan Communist Party, was killed in combat. Then on 25 July, an Army patrol captured three FULNA guerrillas, including a woman, in the area between Polilla Hill and Guasú Hill, in the Yvyturusú range, and they were immediately killed.

On 9 August, Paraguayan Army troops captured and killed another group of guerrillas near the city of Coronel Bogado, who were trying to reach the Paraná River to return to Argentina. The final defeat of the *Ytororó* column came on 10 August, when all the remaining rebels and their commanders, ex-Air Force Lieutenant Adolfo Ávalos Carísimo and Norberto Martínez, were killed in combat in the Cerro Guasú area, Itapúa. According to witnesses, the mutilated bodies of the guerrillas were thrown into the Paraná River or dumped in bags from Air Force aircraft in the middle of the surrounding forests. This was denied by the Minister of the Interior, Edgar L. Ynsfrán, who only admitted that several captured guerrillas were airlifted to the Guairá Government Delegation, to be interrogated and then taken to military prisons.

In less than two months, the counterinsurgency operations had killed 52 guerrillas, some of them in combat but the majority under torture, of the 54 who originally entered Paraguay, including three women. After such catastrophic losses, the General Secretary of the PCP, Oscar Creydt, ordered the suspension of all further guerrilla activity. With the termination of the guerrilla struggle, the PCP emphasised the expansion of its political work with peasants, indoctrinating them with communist dogma so that they themselves, when the time came, could rise up against the Paraguayan government.

After the annihilation of the *Ytororó* column, Creydt abandoned the *foquismo* ('to focus') method created by Che Guevara and ordered the members of the *Mariscal López* column to instead

A Paraguayan Army platoon in full gear, with M1 helmets and M1 Garand rifles, moments before being airlifted to the zone of operations in 1960. (Ejército Paraguayo)

follow the Chinese strategy of prolonged war, which consisted of keeping a very low profile, making the peasants aware of communist ideas and establishing a base in the hills near the town of Acahay. The FULNA continued in essence, while the guerrilla withdrawal helped the group to accumulate strength. The guerrilla command thus received orders not to carry out further military actions, but to instead perform armed propaganda tasks. The *Mariscal López*

One of the Paraguayan Army's Dodge WC51 trucks struggling through the thick Alto Paraná forest in 1960. (Ejército Paraguayo)

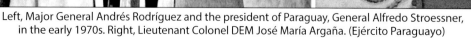

Left, Major General Andrés Rodríguez and the president of Paraguay, General Alfredo Stroessner, in the early 1970s. Right, Lieutenant Colonel DEM José María Argaña. (Ejército Paraguayo)

column thus continued to expand the extent of the territory where it was active.

At the beginning of November 1960, a group of 10 guerrillas appeared in the Alto Paraná area, pursued and attacked not only by Colorado militia but also by personnel of Cavalry Regiment Nr. 1 *Valois Rivarola*, whose base was 7km from the city of Puerto Presidente Stroessner, under the command of Major Adolfo Samaniego. Upon learning of these events, the Minister of the Interior flew in a TAM C-47 piloted by Captain Epifanio Cardozo, who carried out an aerial reconnaissance of the area of influence of the guerrilla group but was unable to locate them due to the density of the forest. The C-47 landed at the air strip in the town of Yhú, from where the persecution of the rebels was organised.

The guerrillas killed two members of the Colorado militia, Raúl Arsenio Oviedo and Moisés Villalba, both leaders of the Colorado Party from the town of Yhú. With the arrival in the area of the *Valois Rivarola* troops, a search was undertaken for the guerrillas, who were found after a few days and killed in combat in the Yvyrarovaná forests.

Meanwhile, as the anti-guerrilla struggle was being carried out, a minor military crisis broke out involving rival groups within the armed forces. A small group led by the commander of the cavalry, Colonel Sixto Duré Franco, which also included General Cáceres, Colonel Fretes Dávalos, General Patricio Colmán and Chief of Police Colonel Ramón Duarte Vera, got together to talk about the possibility of carrying out a coup against General Stroessner, having found out that several officers, including Major Andrés Rodríguez, commander of Cavalry Regiment Nr. 3, and Major José María Argaña, the president's military aide, were allegedly smuggling whiskey and cigarettes. This provoked anger among some of the high-ranking officers, but the plot was discovered almost immediately and thwarted. The leader of the group, Duré Franco, was removed from his post and the rest were 'cordially' invited to remain loyal.

Thus, a potential uprising was quelled long before it was born, and many of the conspirators continued in their posts. José María Argaña, who was a civil pilot, was killed in an airplane accident in the mid-1960s, but Andrés Rodríguez – who like Argaña was then promoted to lieutenant colonel – supposedly continued with his illegal activities, first smuggling goods and later drug trafficking. Stroessner would pay dearly for turning a blind eye to his actions. Rodríguez reached the rank of major general in the 1970s and was later the commander of the entire cavalry force, the most powerful unit of the Paraguayan Army. On 2 February 1989, General Rodríguez, with the support of almost all the armed forces, would lead a coup against Stroessner, which removed him from office after almost 35 years in power. Such are the ironies of fate.

On 5 December 1960, Paraguay broke diplomatic relations with Cuba, accusing the Castro regime of supporting the guerrilla movements of Alto Paraná. At the end of that year, FULNA leader Wilfrido Álvarez, who was responsible for the guerrilla work of the peasant front, organised a group of peasants in the Huguá Rey area, near the town of General Aquino. This group took the city halls of the towns of General Aquino and Itacurubí del Rosario, capturing quantities of armaments in both places while suffering only one casualty, before disappearing back into the forest. The group survived for a long time before it was finally captured and eliminated by a group of police officers led by the Head of the Police Investigation Department, Pastor Coronel, in 1970. Over a period of a couple of years, the FULNA made a series of minor incursions in the nearby area, but due to leadership problems, together with the isolation and harsh living conditions in the forest, the operability of the group was reduced to a minimum. Problems caused by the dual leadership, the bureaucracy of sending messages from the PCP headquarters in Buenos Aires through the regional committee of Asunción, and the decisions made by politicians who had no idea of the daily conditions that the guerrillas faced in the field of operations, froze almost all the activities of the *Mariscal López* column for a long time.

Another problem was that, for security reasons, the communist leaders did not authorise the movement of the *Mariscal López* column camp. The demoralisation thus caused by the isolation and difficult living conditions gave rise to internal disputes between members of the column.

It was at this time that a group from the *Mariscal López* column headed by Ávalos Ocampos carried out an exploration in the San Joaquín mountain range in Caaguazú, in order to establish a possible guerrilla sanctuary. However, the plan was soon discarded since the region was populated by indigenous people who could alert the authorities, as had already happened in other areas.

Starting in 1961 and in order to counteract the FULNA influence on the peasantry, the hierarchy of the Paraguayan Catholic Church, through Caritas Internationalis and the United States Embassy in Paraguay, under a programme known as the 'Alliance for Progress', distributed canned food surpluses of the Korean War and second-hand American clothes to the peasants of many communities, mainly in the Departments of Cordillera and Paraguarí. This was carried out in order to ideologically confront communism and decisively influence the peasants. Meanwhile, members of the Third Franciscan Order acted in working groups to open or improve neighbourhood roads. This was the most immediate antecedent of the Christian Agrarian Leagues and sought to counteract the growth of the revolutionary peasant movement. The first Agrarian Leagues were created in 1962 and 1963 in the area of influence of the

Measures to counter the communist influence of the FULNA included the 'Alliance for Progress' programme of the Kennedy administration, which involved the distribution of aid to poor peasants through Caritas Internationalis and the Third Franciscan Order of the Catholic Church. (Public Domain)

FULNA guerrillas. These leagues would later be the subject of a huge repression by the regime because the government authorities linked them with communist activities.

President Stroessner, with support and a loan from both the United States and the government of the Brazilian president Kubitschek, managed to build a road connecting the city of Coronel Oviedo to the east, to Puerto Presidente Stroessner, with the aim of integrating Paraguay with Brazil and allowing the colonisation of the Caaguazú and Alto Paraná regions by landless peasants. The objective was to reduce the pressure of the peasant movement against the government, probably under advice from the American Embassy. The peasants had certainly been pressing for a piece of land to call their own, but the conditions offered by the new 'colonisation' were not the best since the areas involved were at the time covered with impenetrable forests. Nevertheless, the government offered land to peasants from the Cordillera, Paraguarí and Central areas in an attempt to move them away from the FULNA zones of influence.

In April 1961, Fidencio Pérez, a Colorado Party leader who was labelled the 'strongest bandit and criminal' by the FULNA, was captured and executed by the *Mariscal López* column. Incredibly, the author of that assassination was another Colorado leader, Pablo Cabral, the mayor of the city of Piribebuy, who was a friend of the communist leader Arturo López.

At the end of December 1961 and in early January 1962, FULNA member retired Naval NCO Felipe Nery Alcaraz was actively participating in a plan to hijack the Paraguayan Navy survey boat *Suboficial Rogelio Lesme*, on which he had previously served as a radio operator. That boat was deployed to patrol the area around Yacyretá Island in the Paraná River, and the plan was to take it by force and then make an attempt on the life of President Stroessner, who used to go fishing in the area. To carry out the plan, Alcaraz contacted another former Navy radio operator, retired NCO Francisco Ortíz, also a FULNA member. Along with others, they would crew a boat for the attack on the Navy vessel. From a radio station in the city of Ituzaingó in Argentina, the pair sent a series of messages simulating official orders from the Navy Command (COMAR) for the boat to leave its station and carry out a patrol in the middle of the river. Once there, the insurgents' boat would move closer and those aboard would take the *Suboficial Rogelio Lesme* by assault. However, the plan did not work out due to a lack of coordination, as when the rebels arrived at the scene the Navy boat had already left.

Political and military training in Cuba continued during 1962 for some 16 Paraguayans from the opposition parties, Communists, Liberals and Febreristas, but many of them were arrested by the

The 'Friendship Bridge' between Brazil and Paraguay was inaugurated in 1965. Note the impenetrable forests on the Paraguayan side of the border at the top of the photo. (Public Domain)

police upon their return to Paraguay and under torture revealed the names of others who had been in Cuba. In July, Oscar Creydt, the General Secretary of the PCP, in a report on the national situation and the work of the party, addressed the economic crisis (company closures, famine and exorbitant loans), the political crisis (the failure of the attempt to reorder the old voter registration system for the election in 1963), the workers who had mobilised in a bid for salary increases, the student struggles in May and the sugarcane

The Navy survey boat *Suboficial Rogelio Lesme* (LPH01), which is still in service with the Paraguayan Navy today. (Armada Paraguaya)

worker protests that year. Creydt also saluted the triumph of the left wing of the Febrerista Revolutionary Party, whose president, Benigno Perrota, had declared himself in favour of the formation of a democratic front that encompassed all movements (the M14-V and FULNA) along with all parties and organisations.

In 1962 and 1963, a system of passage for people with mail for guerrilla commanders was being organised in different parts of the country, the most important area being from the confluence of the Pilcomayo and Paraguay Rivers to the ports of Itá Enramada, Asunción and San Antonio. Many mail carriers were captured by the police or military, so the passage system was constantly having to be reorganised.

On 8 June 1963, one of the rebels' main leaders, Wilfrido Álvarez, was having what was believed to be a secret meeting with Celso Ávalos, Idalina Gaona and Arturo López, all members of his cell, in a house in the Pinozá neighbourhood of Asunción. Álvarez was in charge of the Peasant Front and the FULNA's military organisation. Despite the supposed secrecy, the house was surrounded by police officers, who ordered all those inside to surrender. Receiving no response, the police attacked the house. Álvarez told his comrades to flee since they only had a single gun, which he used to fatally wound Police Inspector Commissioner Miguel A. Abdala. According to the official version of events, Álvarez, before being captured, committed suicide, but it is believed that he was probably killed by the police during the assault on the house. The other three rebels were able to escape. After Álvarez's death, Arturo López left the country due to an illness, receiving treatment abroad, as later did Ávalos Ocampos, who was suffering from acute anaemia. Meanwhile, Romilio López remained in hiding in charge of the *Mariscal López* column.

In October 1963, the Central Committee of the PCP decided to dissolve the FULNA, leaving its remaining 17 active members extremely discouraged. To calm the situation, Arturo López was sent to the Soviet Union to undertake various courses and receive further training in February 1964. At the end of 1963, the PCP sent new commanders for the *Mariscal López* column, Santiago Coronel Acevedo (alias Cibils), who had been trained in Czechoslovakia to manufacture landmines, and Blas Alvarenga Caballero (alias Patricio) and Andrés García Valiente (alias Tomás), who were trained in Cuba.

Rather than getting stronger, the hard life of the guerrillas in the forest was weakening them both physically and mentally. The lack of food, shoes, clothing and essential elements such as tents and hammocks made their lives miserable. Consequently, there were several important defections and internal struggles over leadership issues.

In 1962 and 1963, the FULNA prepared another column, the *Rodríguez de Francia* (José Gaspar Rodríguez de Francia was one of the heroes of Paraguayan independence in 1811 and later Supreme Dictator of the government between 1814 and 1840), in the city of Campo Grande in the Brazilian state of Mato Grosso do Sul. Its leader was former Paraguayan Army Lieutenant Colonel Lorenzo Abel López Arrúa, who had joined the PCP after the military uprising of 9 June 1946 against the pro-Nazi military of the 'War Front' of the government of General Higinio Morínigo. López Arrúa had been a member of the PCP ever since and had even befriended Che Guevara. That friendship was crucial to obtain funds from Cuba to sponsor the FULNA. Another leader was the former Paraguayan Army sapper Lieutenant Gaspar Alex Barrett. Members of this group moved to a new headquarters in the city of Itapecerica da Serra, in the state of São Paulo, in 1963. The original plan was for them to enter Paraguay through the city of Pedro Juan

Arturo López Areco, alias Agapito Valiente, the FULNA commander of the *Mariscal López* column. (Policía Nacional)

Four FULNA effectives of the *Mariscal López* column, posing for a picture in a forest in 1961. (Policía Nacional)

Caballero, in Amambay, reaching the department of Cordillera, where they would meet up with the *Mariscal López* column. Everything was almost ready when, on 31 March 1964, a military coup deposed Brazilian president João Goulart. The new military authorities, led by President Marshal Humberto de Alencar Castelo Branco, soon became aware of the Paraguayan guerrillas in Brazil and decided to disrupt them before they could begin to operate. Army troops seized the apartments of FULNA leaders and arrested them. Documents and weapons were also seized and the group was abruptly disbanded. All the information thus obtained was later shared with the Paraguayan government.

In May 1963, the Presidency of the Republic of Paraguay acquired a brand-new twin-engine Cessna 310H, which received the civil registration ZP-TDR. This aircraft was extensively used by President Stroessner on his trips within the country. It was also used by ministers with executive power and commanders of large military units. Although a civilian aircraft, the Cessna 310H was always crewed by Air Force pilots. Stroessner later also used the De

There was an attempt to create yet another FULNA column in 1964, which would be called the *Mariscal Estigarribia* (General José Félix Estigarribia was the Commander-in-Chief of the Paraguayan Army during the Chaco War), whose leader would have been Mariano Reyes, but he was captured by the Army before he was able to put his plan in motion.

During 1964, the police arrested numerous urban FULNA collaborators. Detailed information about these collaborators was usually only obtained through long sessions of torture. Meanwhile, the leadership crises deepened with the PCP. Within the Paraguayan Communist Party, whose top

Brazilian President Marshal Humberto de Alencar Castelo Branco, who remained in power from 1964–67). President Castelo Branco is shown with his Paraguayan counterpart Alfredo Stroessner upon the inauguration of the 'Friendship Bridge' across the Paraná River on 27 March 1965. (Public Domain)

Havilland DH-104 Dove, serial T-39, which had been donated by Argentina on 15 August 1962, but he actually preferred to fly in a comfortable TAM C-47.

In March 1964, a huge COIN operation by the Army around the city of Piribebuy led to the capture of not only most of the FULNA fighters there but also the peasants who supported the guerrillas logistically. Very few members of the *Mariscal López* column managed to escape, having tried unsuccessfully to steal armaments in order to continue the fight. Meanwhile, hundreds of peasants were arrested in the departments of Paraguarí and Cordillera, accused of cooperating with the guerrillas. At a press conference, the Minister of the Interior, Edgar L. Ynsfrán, officially announced the destruction of the FULNA. The success of the government against the rebel group had mainly been due to the infiltration of police agents among newly recruited FULNA members in 1963.

leaders were exiled in Buenos Aires, there were two well-defined groups: one pro-Soviet that prioritised direct armed struggle, and another pro-Chinese, which gave greater importance to long-term indoctrination to workers and peasants. Discussions were endless and an agreement was never reached. As a consequence of this divided leadership, those guerrillas who were still active in the forests suffered numerous hardships.

In September 1964, the commander of the *Mariscal López* column, Celso Ávalos Ocampos, alias Dionisio, had to leave the country due to being seriously ill with acute anaemia. In Buenos Aires he met Oscar Creydt, informing him about the progress of events in Paraguay. Once Dionisio had recovered, he was formally invited to visit the Soviet Union, together with Arturo López and Romilio López, to receive further training. Meanwhile, sub-commander Romilio López, obeying the general secretary's summons, was transported by

The Paraguayan Air Force De Havilland DH-104 Dove, serial T-39, donated by Argentina in 1962 to be used as a presidential plane. (Fuerza Aérea Paraguaya)

The Minister of the Interior, Dr Edgar L. Ynsfrán, pictured during a press conference, showing a captured FULNA mortar bomb in 1964. (Dr. Ynsfrán Archives)

his brother-in-law on a motorcycle to the border, but police officers had set up a barrier at the Ypacaraí toll office on Route Nr. 2 in a bid to capture him, López's relative having previously alerted the police about the trip in return for money. When the pair approached the police barrier, the rider jumped off his motorbike and fled, leaving the guerrilla at the mercy of the police. Romilio was unarmed and tried to escape, but he was quickly captured after a short fight. The police then took him to the Investigation Department, where he was savagely tortured for 22 days, but incredibly, he did not reveal the names of any of his comrades. He was not heard of again, so it is assumed that he died in captivity.

Despite all the rebels' recent setbacks, the beginning of 1965 saw an extraordinary growth in the bases of the so-called *Frente Campesino* (Peasant Front), supported by the FULNA, in various cities and towns of the interior of Paraguay. This did not go unnoticed by the government, which had infiltrators in all the meetings to obtain information about future actions and, above all, identify the leaders. Despite the directives of the PCP, the still active

FULNA guerrillas made sporadic incursions into ranches to steal animals for their survival, and to small towns, where they attacked police detachments to take their weapons, before immediately retreating into the forest. As a consequence of these actions, police detachments in the local countryside were reinforced with more personnel, appropriately armed to repel any attack by the guerrillas. Three months before the great repression, military training began with the new sympathisers at dawn on the banks of the Yhaguy River. The 29-strong group received training in guerrilla warfare, under the supervision of FULNA leader Antoliano López. They were taught attack manoeuvres, methods of progressive advance, crawling on the ground, how to cross estuaries, techniques to throw hand grenades and hand-to-hand combat.

On 15 June 1965, the government began a repressive wave around the city of Caacupé, where several FULNA collaborators were arrested and taken to various police stations in Asunción. They were subjected to torture to reveal the names of other members and the group's plans. Many of the collaborators died as a result of torture, and those who survived spent many years in prison. Some managed to escape and obtain asylum in various embassies around the capital. With the information obtained, the police mounted an operation in the Santa Elena area. To serve as an example, when they captured a leader, they took him to the town's public square and then beat him in front of the local population. Similar procedures were carried out in the cities of Itacurubí, Santa Elena, Sapucai, Escobar and Piribebuy. A price was also put on the heads of the FULNA leaders. Consequently, the guerrilla Santiago Coronel Acevedo, alias Cibils, was captured on 30 July in the vicinity of La Pastora and immediately killed.

The regime's repression extended to all opposition political parties, even to Colorado dissidents, and also to the FREDE (Revolutionary Democratic Student Front), whose members were high school and university students. They were forced to work in the Tacumbú quarry from their prison in the Police Security Guard base in Asunción.

On 30 August 1965, the Stroessner regime organised ceremonies in four districts in the department of Cordillera, in the presence of numerous residents of the area, in which groups of peasants who had been accused of collaborating with the FULNA were 'rebaptised' by priests of the Catholic Church after publicly renouncing Satan and communism. By doing so, many of them saved their lives, but life was still not easy for them afterwards as their neighbours, relatives and friends refused any contact with them.

Incredibly, a small group of the *Mariscal López* column managed to survive the cruel repressions of 1964 and 1965. They remained in their zone of influence in the forests for almost five more years, with almost no logistical support. During all that time, the communist leader Arturo López Areco, alias Agapito

Army troops being deployed to the Cordillera area in 1964 to fight against FULNA members of the *Mariscal López* column. (Ejército Paraguayo)

The Minister of the Interior, Dr Edgar L. Ynsfrán (third from the right), posing with military personnel and local peasants, showing the FULNA armaments seized in 1964. (Dr. Ynsfrán Archives)

Some former FULNA collaborators swearing on the Bible to renounce and abhor communism and Satan in a public event organised by the government on 30 August 1965. (Policía Nacional)

Paraguayan Army Brigadier General Patricio Colmán. (Ejército Paraguayo)

Valiente, had become a legend, an example to follow among the FULNA guerrillas. He was born in the rural area of Ka'undy near the city of Barrero Grande (the present city of Eusebio Ayala) in 1920 and became a schoolteacher in 1945. He joined the Paraguayan Communist Party in the 1940s. A natural leader, he convinced many peasants to join the PCP. He joined the rebels in the revolution of 1947 to fight against the government but was captured and sent to prison. After that conflict, the PCP was outlawed and began to operate underground. After being released in 1949, he went to the Cordillera region to inculcate peasants with communist ideals, in addition to teaching them to read and write, since most of them were illiterate.

In 1958, the Central Committee of the PCP commissioned Arturo López to organise a peasant defence group, which would be the seed of the FULNA *Mariscal López* column. When the FULNA was founded, he became an active member. During the guerrilla operations, he managed not to be detained, leaving the country on several occasions. He managed to get in touch with their comrades in the woods and even travel abroad in the trunk of a car. On 17 May 1970, he was travelling in this manner in a car driven by his cousin, Blas Cristaldo, who had previously reported him to the authorities. The car was intercepted by Army troops on Route Nr. 2, near Guy Hill in the district of the city of Ypacaraí, and forced to stop. General Colmán himself was there with several troops of Infantry Regiment Nr. 14 for the historic arrest of the communist leader. Colmán opened the trunk of the car and was immediately wounded by Arturo López, who was killed by the general's escort. Colmán was quickly evacuated to the military hospital in Asunción, where his wound was treated. His convalescence was slow and painful, and he never fully recovered. Two years later, in August 1972, he would die of complications from his injuries at Walter Reed Army

Indigenous people of the Paĩ-Tavyterã ethnic group, who served as guides for the Paraguayan Army operations against the guerrilla groups in the deep forests. They are posing in army uniforms, although they were not enlisted as regular troops. The one in a dark suit was Chief 'Captain' Juan Pablo Vera. (Ejército Paraguayo)

Paraguayan Army War School professors, pictured in 1959, from left to right, Lieutenant Colonel Duarte Redes, Colonel Alborno, Colonel Frutos, Colonel Bejarano, Major General Ramos Giménez (War School Director), Colonel Bóveda, Colonel Garcete and Colonel Ortíz Molinas. (Ejército Paraguayo)

(a Uruguayan), none of them with ties to the FULNA – were sent from Montevideo in Uruguay to Paraguay to carry out the mission. The date of the attack was set for during the celebrations of 15 August, the Day of Asunción, a national holiday in Paraguay. The mercenaries arrived on the Argentinian shore of the Paraguay River and decided to hire a canoeist, Oscar C. Portillo, to cross the river, offering him very good pay. Even though Portillo was highly suspicious of the intention of his passengers, the crossing was done during the night. However, once they landed on Paraguayan territory

Medical Center (WRAMC) in Washington DC, where he had gone for surgery and better treatment than could be obtained in Paraguay.

The PCP, despite everything, wanted to assassinate President Stroessner at any cost. Thus, in August 1970, four mercenaries – Horacio Marcos Cano and Juan José Ávila (who were Argentines), Salam Ibrain Mesconi (an Arab) and Darío Gilberto Goñi Martínez

and started walking into the forests, Portillo reported them to the Paraguayan Coast Guard commander of the area, Navy Captain Inocencio Acosta López, who together with several Navy and police personnel soon captured the four mercenaries.

The resounding failure of the FULNA in the armed struggle resulted in the division of the PCP. Several leaders decided to found

Paraguayan armed forces students of the War School in 1959. Front row, from left to right, Major Samaniego (commander of Cavalry Regiment Nr. 1), Major Fretes Dávalos (commander of the Presidential Escort Battalion), Navy Commander Hugo González (General Prefect of the Coast Guard), Colonel Bóveda (War School professor), Lieutenant Colonel Sixto Duré Franco (Commander of Cavalry Division Nr. 1), Major Andrés Rodríguez (commander of Cavalry Regiment Nr. 3) and Major Ortiz (commander of the Army Signal Corps). Second row, from left to right, Major Irala (Adjutant of the Army Logistics Corps), Major Gerardo Johannsen (commander of the Air Regiment of the Air Force), Mayor Solís (commander of Cavalry Regiment Nr. 2), Major Martínez (commander of the Artillery Regiment), Major PAM René Zotti (Chief of the Air Department of the Air Force), Major Prieto Busto (commander of the Cadet Corps of the Military School) and Major José María Argaña (Presidential Aide). Third row, from left to right, Major Palacios (Commander of the Cavalry Regiment Nr. 4), Major Toñanez (Adjutant of the War Material Corps), Major Centurión (Chief of the Army Department), Major PAM Adrián Jara (Air Force Chief of Staff), Major Zapattini (Army Artillery commander) and Major PAM Vicente Quiñones (Director of Civil Aeronautics). (Ejército Paraguayo)

Paraguayan Air Force North American AT-6C Texan pilots Lieutenant PAM Gómez Puig
(left) and Lieutenant PAM Nicolás Aparicio. (Fuerza Aérea Paraguaya)

another communist party, the Paraguayan Leninist Communist Party (PCLP), in open opposition to Creydt, blaming him for having an autocratic and intolerant style of leadership. In 1967, with the approval of the Soviet Union, Oscar Creydt was expelled from the PCP on charges of treason, having an inflated ego and mental instability. The PCLP was then dissolved, and its leaders returned to the PCP. Creydt went on to found his own pro-Chinese party, which he called the *Partido Comunista del Paraguay*.

The failure of the FULNA guerrillas was fundamentally due to the fact that they were poorly equipped, had little or no military training, inadequate and old weapons – many of which proved useless – rations for only a few days and a lack of logistical support and guides in the territory where they operated. Some of the rebels had grown up in cities and were not used to the harsh conditions of the forest, which explains why there were numerous defections in a very short time. The FULNA, like the M14-V, proved unable to forge strong ties with the masses, having practically no popular support. They were alone against powerful armed forces. Another crucial

factor in their defeat was that the communist leaders underestimated the military power of the Paraguayan Army, Navy and Air Force.

Although the PCP leaders gave precise instructions to the guerrillas to abandon the typical Che Guevara tactics of high mobility and self-sufficiency, to focus instead on the Chinese strategy of prolonged war based on slow insertion in peasant communities to spread communist ideas, this was not accepted by the FULNA insurgents, who wanted to carry out a quick campaign, fighting in the Cuban style.

Another factor that led to the failure of the guerrilla group was the enormous delay in decision-making by the PCP leadership, which was far away in Buenos Aires, with crucial decisions not being taken by the commanders on the battlefield. Two other issues that played against the effectiveness of the FULNA was the group's ignorance of the complexity of the Paraguayan peasant culture and underestimation of the Stroessner regime's military power and its ability to infiltrate agents within the PCP.

It is estimated that 250 *guerrilleros* were killed between 1959 and 1965, whereas the Paraguayan Army, according to official sources,

The Paraguayan government purchased three Consolidated Vultee PBY-5A Catalinas in 1955. One of them was destroyed in a fatal accident in the US before delivery, but the other two eventually made it to Paraguay and were jointly used by LATN and TAM. One of the Catalinas, ZP-CBB/T-31, was destroyed in an accident in 1957. (Fuerza Aérea Paraguaya)

Above, the Paraguayan Chief of Police, Brigadier General Ramón Duarte Vera (in a dark suit), with high-ranking officers in 1965 at the Police HQ in Asunción. Below left, in the 1950s and early 1960s, police officers used salacot helmets, which were replaced by M1 versions in the late 1960s. (Policía Nacional)

suffered only nine casualties: Cavalry Lieutenant Moisés Galeano, who was killed in the Palomares Ranch, near the town of Yhú on 28 November 1960, and eight soldiers, Rufino Aguilar (Infantry Regiment Nr. 14), Adriano Ramírez, Claudio Aguilar and Pedro Ramírez (of the Police Security Guard), and Ceferino Romero Landaida, Onofre Arzamendia, Ceferino Denis Melgarejo and Emiliano López Irala (from Cavalry Regiment Nr. 1). However, unofficially, it is estimated that the anti-insurgency forces had around 50 casualties, including killed and wounded. Many of the casualties were the consequences of booby traps set by the guerrillas in the middle of the thick forests. In his memoirs, former Minister of the Interior Edgar L. Ynsfrán recognised the latter estimate as correct.

5

THE OPM AND THE CHRISTIAN AGRARIAN LEAGUES (LAC)

In the mid-1970s, the Stroessner regime was in full swing. It had achieved some democratic features, since the parliament by then had several members of the opposition (from the Liberal Party and Febrerista Revolutionary Party).

In the socioeconomic field, a boom was created by the construction of the Itaipú Dam and by major agro-export investments, with an average annual GDP growth of 10 percent until at least 1983. A new bourgeoisie and middle class were being formed, its members being very enthusiastic about the economic benefits of the regime, but indifferent to the absence of certain freedoms and the violation of human rights.

The 'democracy without communism' regime still had the unconditional support of the Republican administration of US president Gerald Ford. The entire region was dominated by governments that shared the 'National Security Doctrine'. The Itaipú Treaty was signed in 1973 with the military government in Brazil led by General Ernesto Geisel, while there was a political-military dictatorship in Uruguay headed by President Juan María Bordaberry and General Hugo Banzer in Bolivia from 1971. Only the Argentine government, headed by Isabel Perón, had certain freedoms, but that was about to change.

However, two internal sources of opposition remained in Paraguay, which would be pre-emptively annihilated by the Stroessner regime in 1976 without receiving internal or external criticism. With the leaders of both factions of the Communist Party being imprisoned or assassinated, a 'new left' was emerging in the Independent Movement of the universities in the capital and among some leaders of the Agrarian Leagues in the interior of the country. In addition, a sector of the Catholic Church, politically sensitised after the Conference of Latin American Bishops of Medellín, Colombia, in 1968, had its progressive teachers among the Jesuits of Paraguay.

The 'new left' had no connection with the Communist Party and was very critical of the opposition from the traditional parties, which had legitimised the Stroessner regime with the 1967 Constitution and in the parliament.

The OPM's armed struggle was centred in a regional context of a group of young guerrillas of Marxist-Leninist inspiration, who in the 1960s and 1970s sought to overthrow right-wing military governments through armed struggle: the Tupamaros in Uruguay; the *Ejército Revolucionario del Pueblo* (ERP) and the *Montoneros* in Argentina; the *Ação Libertadora Nacional* (ALN), *Ação Popular* (AP), *Comando de Libertação Nacional* (COLINA), *Grupos de Once* (Gr-11), *Movimento Revolucionário 8 de Outubro* (MR-8), *Resistência*

Catholic priest Father Braulio Maciel, in charge of the Jejuí parish in the 1970s. (Diario Ultima Hora)

Four leaders of the OPM, from left to right, Juan Carlos Da Costa (founder of the organisation), José Félix Bogado Tabackman, Nidia Antonina González Talavera and Mario Schaerer Prono. (Policía Nacional)

Armada Nacionalista (RAN), *Vanguarda Armada Revolucionaria-Palmares* (VAR Palmares) and *Vanguarda Popular Revolucionária* (VPR) in Brazil; and the *Guerrilla de Ñancahuazú* of Che Guevara in Bolivia.

Culturally, this new generation was the daughter of global and regional processes such as that of May 1968 in Paris and the great protest known as the *Cordobazo*, a popular insurrection that occurred in the city of Córdoba, Argentina, against the military government on 29 and 30 May 1969. In Paraguay, the movement began in June 1969 during protests against the visit of US government special envoy Nelson Rockefeller. Many Paraguayan university students had been 'trained' politically at the universities of La Plata and Corrientes in Argentina, and also in Santiago de Chile.

It was in Chile, during the rule of the socialist government of Salvador Allende, that the project of the Political-Military Organisation (OPM) emerged. In 1973, several Paraguayan citizens were studying either economics or sociology at Chilean universities, including the brothers José Félix and Eduardo Bogado Tabackman, Diego Abente, Víctor Hugo Ramos and Melquiades Alonso. During that year, before the military coup of 11 September, the man who would go on to be the undisputed leader of the OPM, Juan Carlos Da Costa, then 27 years old, contacted the Paraguayan students. He had been imprisoned and tortured in Paraguayan jails in the various repressions against the Agrarian Leagues. From their meetings, the consensus emerged that the 'Chilean path to socialism' through democratic elections was not a viable option for Paraguay, the only alternative being an armed struggle. A short time later, Da Costa also contacted Paraguayan university students in Corrientes, such as Carlos Brañas, Carlos Fontclara and Jorge Zavala, as well as *Montoneros* elements through Carlos Livieres, a Paraguayan member of the Peronist guerrilla movement.

In the two Paraguayan universities, a movement had been growing since the late 1960s that opposed those students of the Colorado Party who wanted to take over all the student unions of

The cover of one of the issues of the OPM magazine *Tatapirirí* in 1975. (Policía Nacional)

the various faculties, especially in the Faculties of Engineering and Medicine of the National University and the Faculty of Philosophy and Human Sciences of the Catholic University, which together with the Literary Academies of several high schools formed the so-called "Independent Movement" (MI).

In 1973, differences arose between the most radical and reformist sectors of the MI, which were accentuated with the arrival of Da Costa and the Paraguayan students in Chile. The following year, the MI had become a prolific hotbed of OPM cadres and militants, joining as leaders Fernando Masi, Mario Schaerer Prono and his wife Guillermina Kanonnikoff, Miguel Ángel López Perito, Carlos Ortíz and Daniel Campos.

Simultaneously and without ties with these university groups in the capital, since 1972 there was a similar split between radicals and reformists in the Christian Agrarian Leagues (LAC) in the interior of the country. These groups had been created at the beginning of the 1960s in the heat of the social doctrine of the Catholic Church, as basic Christian communities similar to those of Brazil and other Latin American countries, under the spiritual leadership of Bishops Helder Cámara, Leonardo Boff, Gustavo Gutierrez and others. Seeking to 'live as brothers' according to evangelical teaching, rural families led by priests committed to social pastoralism and the theology of liberation cultivated common farms in the *minga* system (the solidarity of a group of friends and/or neighbours for some common work) and created community warehouses. Along the pedagogical lines of Paulo Freire, they maintained their own bilingual schools (Spanish-Guaraní), with their own programmes and texts adapted to the peasants' reality.

Soon the government, businessmen, principals of official schools and members of the Colorado Party accused them of being communist. Within a short time, the regime's police and military forces began a brutal repression of these groups, which also extended to the leading priests such as Bishops Aníbal Maricevich and Bogarín Argaña, Father Braulio Maciel and Jesuit priests José Miguel Munárriz, Luis Farré and José Caravias. Between 1965 and 1970, hundreds of members of these leagues from Caaguazú, Cordillera, Concepción, Paraguarí and Misiones were arrested and sent to the capital, where they were tortured and imprisoned. Due to this oppression, many communities abandoned the leagues in the early 1970s and foreign priests linked to the groups were expelled from the country. Some former members of the leagues separated from the tutelage of the clergy of the Catholic Church and began to meet clandestinely in order to plan to confront the violence of the regime with violence of their own. Some of them went to Argentina to receive political and armed struggle training.

Of all the LAC communities, the town of Jejuí was one of the most emblematic for its community practices. In 1975, this settlement was attacked by 120 troops commanded by Army Colonel José F. Grau and a number of Colorado militiamen. Father Braulio Maciel was wounded and around 100 peasants, some American and European officials from cooperation organisations and two Spanish nuns were taken in Army trucks to a prison camp in the area. The leaders were taken to the capital, where they were savagely tortured at the Police Investigations Department. The women and children of the settlement were left in Jejuí but completely surrounded by Army troops, without supplies or medicine for three months. Between April and May of that year, infantry troops carried out a similar procedure in the Colonia Buena Vista near the town of Yhú, in the Caaguazú area, burning huts and crops and taking peasants as prisoners, who were sent to police stations and military bases in the cities of Caaguazú and Villarrica.

The destruction of Jejuí, a peaceful and strongly religious place, and Yhú's harsh repression indirectly strengthened the position of the Agrarian Leagues that planned to resists the regime's violence through armed struggle.

Meanwhile, OPM leader Da Costa had clandestinely returned to Paraguay in 1974. He had been active with the leader of the Agrarian Leagues, Constantino Coronel, and had spent time in prison due to his working with the peasants. Through his partner, Nidia González Talavera, he further strengthened contacts with the group of organised peasants. Months later, the OPM carried out its first and only violent operation when three young leaders tried unsuccessfully to steal a briefcase containing money to pay salaries at the Metropolitan Seminary of the Catholic Church. The victim was slightly injured but managed to hold onto the funds, and the police were not alerted to the incident at the time.

At the end of 1974, some members of the *Montoneros* group entered Paraguay to provide guerrilla and political instruction to young leaders already recruited from the OPM, and in early 1975 a tripartite leadership was structured, involving Da Costa, Nidia González and Coronel. That year, the creation of peasant cells was accelerated in the department of Misiones, and with less intensity in those of Ñeembucú and Paraguarí. With a small press stolen from the Cristo Rey Jesuit School, the OPM edited and distributed 10 issues of the political magazine *Tatapirí*. Each edition had a circulation of 200 copies, and the simple possession of a single copy constituted sufficient police evidence to accuse the student or peasant of being a guerrilla.

The leadership of the OPM drafted a 10-point programme or ideology of nationalistic and revolutionary principles which comprised the following:

1. The consolidation of the political-military organisation
2. The worker-peasant alliance as the fundamental basis of the revolutionary process, with the hegemony of the working class
3. The construction of the revolutionary proletarian party
4. The formation of the Popular Revolutionary Army
5. The prolonged people's war as a general strategy of struggle
6. The formation of the national liberation front
7. Marxism-Leninism as a methodology for analysing reality
8. Revolutionary nationalism
9. Proletarian internationalism
10. Socialism as a historical project

Complex security regulations were set up for the OPM militants, which were not always respected. The organisation was based on cells of a small number of members, which through one of them were connected with the leaders of the columns. Each column, in theory, had 160 members, all previously unknown to each other. If someone was arrested, the code name was to be given to the authorities and not the real name of the other members. However, this organisation never functioned as it should since most of the members knew each other as friends, relatives or university classmates. At the beginning of 1976, only two columns had been partially formed in the capital, while there were some scattered bases in the interior of the country. By then, the OPM was still badly equipped, with just two vans, a handful of motorcycles and a poor arsenal: one machine gun, 30 pistols and revolvers and about 10 rifles. Three properties had been rented as venues for meetings, archives and temporary housing for various leaders. The arsenal of the peasant faction of the OPM, which was based in the department of Misiones, was similarly poor, with only a pair of rifles, one pistol and 15 revolvers.

The OPM was not growing and was unable to incorporate more members in Paraguay, so the leaders contacted Paraguayan students in the city of Corrientes in Argentina who had previously committed to the OPM. Some of them travelled to Paraguay carrying propaganda material, personal guns and documents. The security measures worked well for some time, since for more than two years, militants were enrolled and trained in Asunción and in the interior of the country, their own magazine was published and distributed, and the state security forces were completely unaware of this clandestine organisation. However, the arrest of a member with

Mario Schaerer Prono's police record. The photographs show the lamentable state of the OPM leader perhaps only hours before being killed during sessions of torture. (Policía Nacional)

Three feared members of the Police Investigation Department in the 1970s and 1980s. From left to right, the chief of the department Pastor Coronel and Police Commissioners Camilo Almada and Lucilo Benitez, infamous torturers of the Stroessner regime. (Diarios Ultima Hora and *ABC Color*)

by the OPM and the leaders of the organisation. That same night, police raided the home of peasant leader Martín Rolón in Lambaré, who was killed during a shoot-out. His wife, Estela Jacquet, was arrested and tortured by the police.

The following day, two other members of the OPM possessing a portable press and compromising documents were arrested when they disembarked from the passenger ship *Carlos Antonio López* in the port of Asunción, and another member who had just arrived from Corrientes was captured a few hours later.

At 2:00 a.m. on Monday, 5 April, in a police operation commanded by Commissioner Alberto Cantero, the home of OPM leader Mario Schaerer Prono was raided in the Herrera neighbourhood of Asunción. The house served as the OPM headquarters and was a few blocks from San Cristóbal Church and Parish High School. During the ensuing shoot-out, Commissioner Cantero was injured and the founder of the OPM, Juan Carlos Da Costa, was killed. Schaerer Prono and his wife, Guillermina Kanonnikoff, managed to escape and took refuge in the Parrish High School, where they used to teach. The school principal, an American priest, was Father Raymond Roy. The police soon arrived on the scene, including the feared Chief of Investigations Pastor Coronel, who had been in office since January 1968. After a discussion between the priest and the police chief, who offered guarantees to protect the lives of the couple, Schaerer

compromising materials at the border unleashed a very rapid and forceful repression that destroyed the OPM in less than a month.

On the morning of 3 April 1976, medical student Carlos Brañas, his wife and two other women crossed the Paraná River in a passenger boat, from Posadas in Argentina to Encarnación in Paraguay. During a routine customs search at the Paraguayan border, the police found OPM propaganda material and a firearm in their luggage. Those involved were immediately detained and sent to the Police Investigation Department in Asunción. After several hours of torture, the police extracted information about the premises used

and his wife were handed over to the police. They were taken to the Investigation Department, where Schaerer was tortured so savagely that he eventually died. His wife, who was pregnant, was not physically tortured but was imprisoned. That same night, other members of the OPM, including Diego Abente Brun and his wife and Miguel Ángel López Perito, were also arrested. In another raid in the city of San Lorenzo, the leader of the Agrarian Leagues, Constantino Coronel, was seriously injured. Of all the OPM leaders, only Nidia González Talavera, Da Costa's wife, managed to escape. She was also

Reproduction of the painting called 'Painful Easter' (*Pascua Dolorosa*), made by the Paraguayan communist activist Alberto Barrett, which shows the brutal repression of the regime forces against the peasants of Jejuí in April 1976. (Paraguayan Communist Party newspaper *Adelante*)

pregnant, and months later she gave birth. She managed to leave the country clandestinely.

With some names extracted under torture, Chief of Investigations Pastor Coronel sent Deputy Commissioner Camilo Almada, alias Sapriza, to repress the peasant faction of the OPM in Misiones. With the help of police forces, troops of the Infantry Division Nr. 3 and Colorado militiamen, all the main leaders were arrested and sent to the Abraham-Cué jail in the city of San Juan Bautista. There they were all tortured and many of them murdered in an episode that would later be known as the 'Painful Easter' since it happened during Catholic celebrations of Holy Week of that year. The leaders who lost their lives were Silvano Flores, Diego and Dionisio Rodas, Alejandro Falcón, Ramón Pintos and the brothers Elixto, Policarpo, Francisco and Adolfo López. Hundreds of men and women with some links with these leaders were arrested and tortured too. Other leaders in the Paraguarí area were also captured, tortured and killed by police and the Army Artillery Command personnel. The few possessions

they had were confiscated by government forces and their homes destroyed. The intention was that those actions serve as an example so that other peasants would not dare to help to those who wanted to rebel against the regime.

In this atmosphere of terror, the regime took the opportunity in the following months to repress other 'progressive' groups of the left that had no connection with the OPM. Jesuit priest Miguel Munárriz was arrested, while an arrest warrant was issued against another Jesuit, Father Miguel Sanmartí, who was then residing in Spain, accused of being a leader of the OPM. The police also destroyed all the remaining communities of the Agrarian Leagues, although they were not linked to the armed resistance project.

However, the policy of numerous foreign countries towards events in Paraguay was changing and international organisations for the defence of human rights were already targeting the Paraguayan regime. With the overcrowding of prisoners in the Police Investigation Department, in various police stations and in the Police Security Guard base in Asunción, and under mounting international pressure, more than 1,000 political prisoners, including women, were transferred to the Emboscada Prison (50km from Asunción) in September 1976. This prison was in essence a concentration camp, where communist militants and other left-wing political prisoners were also sent. Two members of the OPM managed to escape to Argentina, but they were kidnapped in Buenos Aires by the Argentine police, under Operation Condor, and handed over to the Paraguayan police.

Almost all members of the OPM in prison were released in 1978, except for Brañas and Gill Ojeda, who remained behind bars for another year. Some would later be detained again and others went into exile, returning to Paraguay only after the 1989 coup d'état that

The chief of the Police Investigation Department, Pastor Coronel (centre), with police personnel in civilian clothes after a raid where a guerrilla was killed (left). A Police GMC patrol truck of the mid-1970s is also shown. (Policía Nacional)

overthrew the regime of General Stroessner. Most of the OPM's militants were poor peasants and its few leaders were university students. Fourteen out of the 17 members of the OPM were executed by the police in April and May 1976. The OPM had its epilogue two years later. At the beginning of 1977, while the entire leadership was still in prison, some leaders who had escaped repression, among them Nidia González, E. Bogado Tabackman and Jorge Zavala, tried to rebuild the OPM and changed its name to *Organización Primero de Marzo* (First of March Organization; 1 March being a holiday in Paraguay when Heroes' Day is celebrated). They repeated the same type of organisation, creating clandestine cells, renting several houses in Asunción to be used as OPM premises, brought arms into the country and republished the magazine *Tatapiriri*.

Bogado Tabackman was arrested in late 1977, and in January 1978 the police arrested and tortured R. Udrizar, a Paraguayan student in Corrientes who had arrived in Asunción. Under torture,

Udrizar revealed the house where another OPM leader, Jorge Zavala, was living clandestinely. The police raided the property and killed Zavala. In their search for evidence and incriminating documents, two commissioners found a trunk and while trying to open it, a booby-trap bomb exploded, wounding both of them. Nevertheless, the police found important documents, including the organisation's future plans and its archives. Another two female leaders of the group took refuge in foreign embassies and managed to leave the country.

Thus, another adventure by left-wing groups of trying to take over the government through an armed struggle ended unsuccessfully. As in the two previous cases in the 1960s, poor training, a tiny number of weapons, lack of popular support and underestimation of the regime's forces played against the OPM, which was swiftly eliminated by the government.

6

THE GOIBURÚ CASE

Agustín Goiburú, who was born in Paraguay on 28 August 1930, studied medicine and specialised in traumatology in Brazil. Upon returning to his native country, Goiburú worked at the Social Security Institute (IPS) and also at the Rigoberto Caballero Police Polyclinic. At the same time, he carried out an active militancy within the Colorado Party, a political group that supported General Alfredo Stroessner. He was a political leader of the Colorado Popular Movement (MOPOCO) and started campaigning against human rights violations committed by the Stroessner regime.

Goiburú, along with other MOPOCO leaders, had to go into exile in 1959, first taking asylum in the Uruguayan Embassy. Later, he settled in the Argentine border city of Posadas, opposite Encarnación in southern Paraguay, where he worked as a doctor. During those years, he complained in the press about the corpses of Paraguayan citizens that appeared floating in the Paraná River, mutilated and with traces of torture, including members of the guerrilla M14-V and FULNA groups who had been captured by the Paraguayan Army. In 1962, Dr Goiburú tried to draw international attention to events in Paraguay by planning the hijacking of a TAM Douglas C-47 at Encarnación Airport to fly to the summit of Latin American foreign ministers at Punta del Este in Uruguay. However, the plan came to the attention of the regime's security forces, who mounted a siege to capture Goiburú and his collaborators, but they miraculously managed to escape.

On 24 November 1969, Goiburú was kidnapped for the first time. He was fishing with his 11-year-old son, Rolando, and some friends in the Paraná River, in Argentine territorial waters, when he was intercepted by a Paraguayan Navy motorboat from the Naval Prefecture based in Encarnación. His boat was towed to the Paraguayan shore and only Rolando was allowed to return to Posadas. Goiburú's friends were imprisoned in the Government Delegation building, the doctor being sent to Asunción by military plane. He was imprisoned in a basement in the Navy headquarters and later sent to several police stations in the capital. While he was detained in the 7th Police Station, he managed to escape through a tunnel on 3 December 1970 and found refuge in the Chilean

Dr Agustín Goiburú (second from the right) in an Argentine police car after being captured in the city of Paraná in 1977. (Policía Nacional)

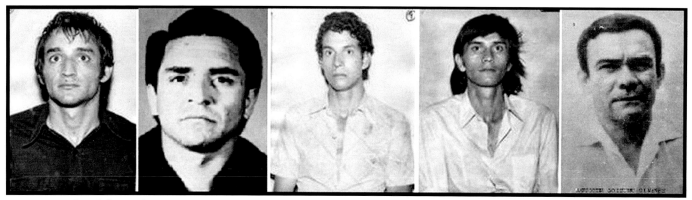

Top, from left to right, Benjamín Ramírez Villalba, Amílcar Oviedo, Carlos Mancuello and Agustín Goiburú. (Policía Nacional)

Embassy. He was able to travel to Chile, but soon returned to Posadas in Argentina.

Convinced that the fall of Stroessner could only be produced by violent methods, in 1974, Dr Goiburú arranged the participation of MOPOCO activists and Paraguayan students at the University of La Plata in Argentina in the carrying out of an attack against the dictator. A van loaded with explosives was to be parked on the route that the dictator usually took near the central railway station in Asunción. However, the operation failed several times, for various reasons, and the perpetrators ended up being discovered by a Navy officer, who had been contacted by one of those involved, Evasio Benítez, to provide him with explosives. The police became aware of the planned attack and immediately captured Benítez, brothers Rodolfo and Benjamín Ramírez Villalba, Carlos Mancuello and

Amílcar Oviedo. They were all tortured and later killed, their bodies never being found.

From then on, Dr Goiburú became Stroessner's public enemy number one. He was, in addition, the great lodestone of the Paraguayan exiles and the only one with the capacity to organise a broad resistance front from Argentine territory. All his movements were watched by a network of spies who kept the Paraguayan security forces informed of his steps. Realising that his personal situation was insecure, Goiburú decided to move to the city of Paraná, far from the Paraguayan border, in March 1975. On 9 February 1977, as part of the infamous Operation Condor, Goiburú was kidnapped by the Argentine police and handed over to their Paraguayan counterparts. He was tortured and killed soon afterwards, and his body was never located.

7

THE 1980 CAAGUAZÚ CASE

The final attempt at a desperate armed protest against General Stroessner's regime took place in the department of Caaguazú in 1980, its protagonists being native peasants from the Misiones region who had already been savagely repressed during the 'Painful Easter' of 1976. When the survivors of the earlier repression were released, they migrated to the Acaray-mí fiscal colony (land belonging to the state but occupied by peasants), which had been created in 1972 on the banks of the Acaray River.

Its leader was Victoriano 'Centú' Centurión, a former prosperous grocer from Caaguazú who, converted to the social doctrine of the Catholic Church, distributed his goods around the Agrarian Leagues. He had spent four years in prison for his membership in the Agrarian Leagues. Centú was legendary among the peasants, who believed that his body was immune to bullets, that he possessed the gift of invisibility and that he heard divine voices of premonition.

The conflict was unleashed when the wife of General Ramos Jiménez claimed possession of the public lands of Acaray-mí, where the colony was based. A military post was installed there to harass the peasants, who were continually detained and forced to carry out work for the military detachment. Due to this harassment, a group of peasants led by Centurión launched a violent protest at the departmental office of the Rural Welfare Institute (IBR) in the city of Caaguazú.

Their action had little hope of success, since the group's arsenal was limited to just two revolvers, two shotguns and 15 large knives,

The *Rápido Caaguazú* bus hijacked by peasants in 1980. (Alcibiades González Delvalle)

and they had no armed training or organised plan to attack the military or police forces. Furthermore, they carried no supplies, water or extra ammunition for guerrilla action, and they knew it was impossible to garner support in the towns along the way or even to survive in the deep forests.

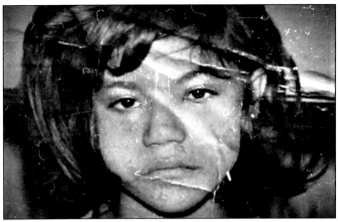

A 12-year-old girl, Apolonia Flores, was with the peasants captured by government forces in March 1980. (Policía Nacional)

In the early morning of 8 March 1980, 20 peasants, including seven minors and three adolescent girls, hijacked a bus belonging to the *Rápido Caaguazú* company 27km from the city of Puerto Presidente Stroessner. They demanded that the driver take them to the city of Caaguazú. After travelling just a few kilometres, the bus crossed a tax checkpoint without stopping; the tax inspectors, believing the occupants of the bus were smugglers, chased after them in two cars. During the chase, the peasants opened fire on the cars, so the inspectors returned to the post to inform the authorities.

When the bus reached the city of Campo 9, the peasants forced the driver to take a local road, reaching a forest, where they remained hidden, waiting for the presumed quick reaction from the government. Indeed, the following morning, troops from Infantry Division Nr. 2, supported by armed Bell OH-13H helicopters of the Paraguayan Air Force and police units led by the Chief of the

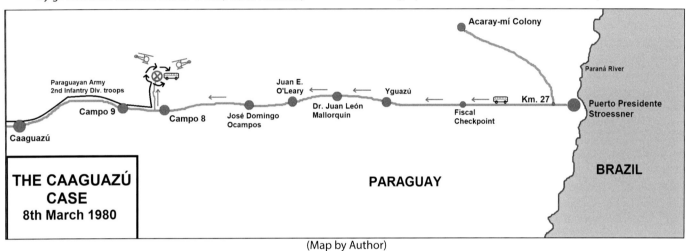

(Map by Author)

Several Paraguayan Air Force armed Bell OH-13Hs were used to locate the peasants who hijacked a bus in March 1980. (Fuerza Aérea Paraguaya)

Infantry Division Nr. 2 troops were also deployed to search for the peasants. (Ejército Paraguayo)

Investigations Department, Pastor Coronel, plus a large number of Colorado militiamen from Campo 9, Juan Manuel Frutos and Caaguazú, arrived in the area and immediately mounted an operation to hunt down the peasants. They were soon located and surrounded by the regime forces to prevent anyone from escaping. Ten out of the 20 peasants were murdered on the spot, the rest being captured. The murdered peasants were Estanislao Sotelo, Mario Ruiz Díaz, Secundino Segovia, Feliciano Verdún, Federico and Reinaldo Gutiérrez, Adolfo César Britos, Concepción González, Fulgencio Castillo Uliambre and Gumercindo Brítez. Two young girls, Apolinaria González and Apolonia Flores, the latter only 12 years old, were wounded and captured, along with seven surviving men from the group. In the following weeks, the Army scoured the departments of Caaguazú and Alto Paraná to search for any more peasants who were involved, especially their leaders. True

to his legend, Victoriano Centurión avoided being captured and most probably killed, and months later he received asylum at the Panamanian Embassy in Paraguay.

Counterinsurgent forces burned crops, looted and destroyed the property of the settlers in Acaray-mí, searching for Centurión for weeks without success. Around Costa Rosado, where the rebel leader was believed to be hiding, military and police forces surrounded the area, which was overflown by Bell OH-13H helicopters. Many peasants were detained and tortured to reveal Centurión's whereabouts, but those captured simply did not know where their leader was. Some 40 peasants were later transferred to the capital, where they continued to be tortured. Some of their number died under torture, others were released, but 14 of them were prosecuted by the regime and sentenced to several years in prison. Six of the latter were released years later after a prolonged hunger strike.

8
THE 1980 OPERATION REPTILE

The last episode of this volume is not related to any of the groups previously described. It was a terrorist attack perpetrated by foreign guerrillas on Paraguayan territory, the Stroessner regime thereafter mobilising both police and military forces to search for them. The attack took place only months after the 'Caaguazú case' described in the previous chapter. The target of the attack was not any government personality or even President Stroessner himself, and unlike the previous guerrilla groups, the intention was not to seize power through an armed struggle, but instead to eliminate a former foreign president who had requested asylum in Paraguay.

Anastasio Somoza Debayle, nicknamed Tachito, was born in León, Nicaragua, on 5 December 1925. He had been the last right-wing dictator of Nicaragua, being the third and final member of the Somoza dynasty, after his father, Anastasio Somoza García, and brother, Luis Somoza Debayle, who had exercised presidential power in Nicaragua since 1937. In the case of Tachito, he served two terms as president of Nicaragua, from 1967–72 and 1974–79. His government and the fight against the socialist Sandinistas are not within the scope of this volume, so only his exile and assassination in Paraguay will be discussed.

Anastasio Somoza Debayle. (1925–80). (Public Domain)

FSLN guerrillas brandishing weapons over a former National Guard tank, surrounded by thousands of supporters, in Managua, the capital of Nicaragua, after Somoza fled the country in 1979. (Bettman)

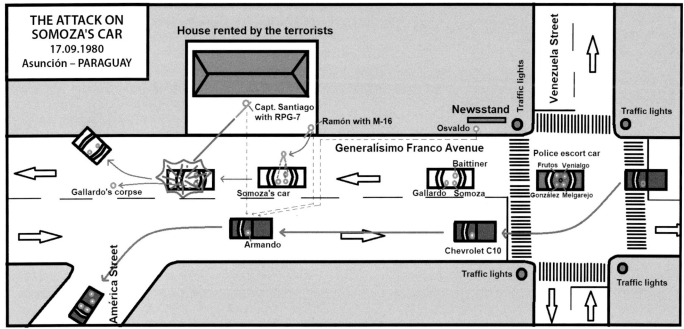

(Map by Author)

The Sandinista National Liberation Front (FSLN) was founded as a left-wing political-military organisation in Nicaragua in 1961 by Carlos Fonseca Amador, Santos López, Tomás Borge, Silvio Mayorga and Germán Pomares Ordóñez, among others. It emerged within the scope of the national liberation movement and proclaimed itself inspired by the nationalist and anti-imperialist legacy of Augusto C. Sandino, from whom it took the name 'Sandinista'. Sandino waged a guerrilla war against the US intervention in Nicaragua between 1927 and 1933, the FSLN members quickly identifying with the Marxist-Leninist ideological trend. In 1979, after a long struggle, the FSLN succeeded in overthrowing the regime of Anastasio Somoza Debayle and the Somoza family dynasty which had ruled Nicaragua for decades.

Due to international pressure from the US government of Democrat Jimmy Carter, the OAS (Organization of American States), along with several other countries, and above all the successful struggle of the FSLN inside Nicaragua, President Somoza presented his unwavering resignation on 16 July 1979. Early in the morning of the following day, at 2:00a.m., a military Sikorsky S-58T helicopter picked up the former president and six of his most faithful collaborators and took them to Managua International Airport. Once there, Somoza and his coterie boarded several executive jets, while other senior officials, commanders of the National Guard and government ministers boarded a LANICA Boeing 727; even two coffins with the remains of Somoza's father and elder brother, who had also been presidents, were loaded on the plane. All aircraft

Colonel Raúl Calvet, LAP's general manager and pilot of Somoza's flight to Asunción (left). Also shown is one of Líneas Aéreas Paraguayas's Boeing 707-321Bs. (Gen. Calvet & Gustavo Figueroa)

headed to Miami. Once there, President Carter let Somoza know that he was not welcome in the United States and urged him to leave as soon as possible. Somoza and collaborators thereafter travelled to the Bahamas, where he was hoodwinked by Prime Minister

Anastasia Somoza in his house in Asunción in 1980. (Public Domain)

Somoza and some of his friends during an expedition to the Chaco in Paraguay in 1980. (Public Domain)

Lynden Pindling, who charged him a million dollars for his stay in that country, only to later deny him asylum. Somoza was forced to leave the Bahamas just two weeks after his arrival. His departure took place in the company of his daughters, Carla and Carolina, son Roberto, 17 guards and various servants. They all headed to Guatemala, whose president, Fernando Romeo Lucas García, arranged the details for Somoza's residence in Paraguay, thanks to his friendship with President Alfredo Stroessner. The Paraguayan president agreed to receive Somoza for reasons of political affinity and because those around Stroessner speculated that they would be able to obtain large amounts of money from their 'guest', as they knew that he had spirited away the Nicaraguan treasury.

On 17 August 1979, the honorary consul of Guatemala in Paraguay, Remigio Bazán Farías, at the request of the Guatemalan government, hired a Boeing 707-321B from Líneas Aéreas Paraguayas (LAP), with its full crew, for a charter flight to Guatemala City, to pick up Somoza and his delegation and bring them to Paraguay. The sum of US$100,000 was paid for the operation.

The LAP crew was made up of the company's general manager, Colonel Raúl Calvet (pilot), Lieutenant Colonel Alcibiades Soto (co-pilot), NCO Juan Pires (flight engineer) and flight attendants Susy Beczko, Irmi Foerster, Verónica Troche, Julio Cáceres and Néstor Arrúa. On 18 August, the LAP jet took off for the eight-hour direct flight to Guatemala City, landing at La Aurora International Airport. The crew waited for two hours while the 707 was refuelled and the 23-strong delegation arrived, headed by the former president, Anastasio Somoza. The party also included General José R. Somoza (Anastasio Somoza's half-brother), Anastasio Somoza Portocarrero (his eldest son), Roberto Somoza Portocarrero (his youngest son), Dinorah Sampson (his lover) and their collaborators Captain José L. Gutiérrez, 2nd Lieutenant Aquiles Cifuentes, Mario Lara, Luis Sirio, Jaime Roa, Abraham

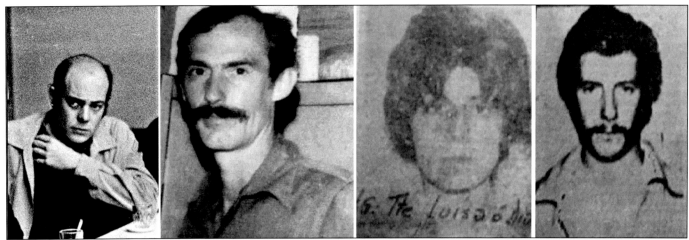

Four of the ERP effectives involved in Operation Reptile: from left to right, Enrique H. Gorriarán Merlo alias "Ramón", Hugo A. Irurzún alias "Capitán Santiago", Silvia Mercedes Hodgers alias "Teniente Hilda/Diana/Julia" and Juan José Pandinni alias "Osvaldo". (Public Domain)

The ERP flag. (Public Domain)

An RPG-7 grenade launcher. (Public Domain)

Gutiérrez, Orlando Poimares, Julio Guerrero, General Rafael Porras, Samuel Ganie Anaya, Roger Sandino, Concepción Sapaldo, Erwin Earl Hooker, Alejandro Montiel, Justo Pastor Rivera, Gerardo Martínez, Alejandro Chavarría and Josefa Matilde Román.

Due to a calculation error, the 707 received more fuel than it needed, so on take-off the overladen aircraft used the entire runway and the rate of climb was very slow, with Colonel Calvet having to perform an evasive manoeuvre to avoid colliding with a radio antenna near the airport. During the return flight, the LAP 707 overflew Peruvian territory. Due to the pressure of time, LAP had not requested the corresponding permits for the flight, and when the aircraft entered Peruvian airspace the local air traffic control ordered the jet to land at the city of Iquitos or it would be intercepted and shot down by the Peruvian Air Force. Colonel Calvet, who had graduated as a military pilot in Peru, had knowledge of the country's military installations and knew that their fighters, whose base was in Arequipa, could not intercept the 707 during its short flight in Peruvian airspace. They therefore immediately silenced all on-board radio communications and headed to Brazil. The flight continued smoothly to Asunción, arriving at its destination at 8:15 p.m. on 19 August.

Somoza settled in a mansion on Mariscal López Avenue and Motta Street in one of the most exclusive neighbourhoods in Asunción, a property that had previously been occupied by the Embassy of South African in Paraguay. During his stay in Paraguay, which lasted a little over a year, he dedicated himself to planning land investments and an active social agenda in clubs, hotels, bars and restaurants. Despite having a lover, Dinorah Sampson, he flirted with various Paraguayan beauty queens and models. His son, Anastasio Somoza Portocarrero, alias Chigüín, got into trouble by flirting with the daughters of several senior military officers. The former Nicaraguan president began to acquire multiple properties

in Paraguay, including 25,000 hectares (at least 8,000 of them were fiscal lands) for cotton cultivation in the department of Misiones, as well as a property in the district of San Cosme y Damián to exploit stones and sell them for the construction of the Yacyretá Dam. Another one of Somoza's plans was to invest in an airline for domestic flights, which failed to materialise. It was also said that he bought a huge farm in Brazil in the state of Goiás, near Brasilia, for US$20 million, as well as coal mines in Colombia and Vision magazine.

Although Somoza could move freely in Paraguay, he always did so with the bodyguards he had brought from Nicaragua, while the Stroessner regime had also assigned him a number of police officers and NCOs for his personal safety, who always accompanied him closely behind in a red Ford Falcon. These police personnel were commanded by Commissioner Francisco Rubén González. Somoza proved to be a major headache for the Paraguayan police, since he never warned his escort about his departures and they continually had to improvise their protection plans. He was warned that for his own safety he should always change his itinerary and the places he frequented, but this was advice that Somoza never paid attention to as he travelled around Paraguay in three cars that he had the use of: a pair of 1978 Mercedes-Benz 250 S-Class saloons – one white and the other blue – and a Jeep Cherokee Chief. This cavalier approach to his own safety would later prove fatal, as it greatly facilitated the work of the terrorists who had him in their sights.

While Somoza and his clique lived a carefree life in Paraguay, investing his fortune in various ventures, former members of the

Minister of the Interior Sabino A. Montanaro (centre with light suit) and Police Investigation Chief Pastor Coronel (centre with dark suit) with other police officers inspecting the remains of Somoza's Mercedes-Benz car after the attack on 17 September 1980. (*Diario ABC Color*)

Police Commissioner Francisco González (left), the head of Somoza's escort, explaining the attack to Investigation Chief Pastor Coronel (right). In the picture on the right, one police commissioner is holding the RPG-7 grenade launcher found at the scene. (*Diario ABC Color*)

The Chevrolet C10 pick-up truck used by the terrorist and abandoned later due to mechanical problems. (*Diario ABC Color*)

FSLN's struggle in Nicaragua for the overthrow of the Somoza regime, so they were comrades in arms. The ERP had been a guerrilla organisation which constituted the military structure of the Marxist-oriented Revolutionary Workers Party (PRT), led by Mario Roberto Santucho, during the 1970s. Towards the beginning of 1977, it was finally dismantled by the military regime in Argentina after Operation Independence and the repressive actions of the government.

Towards the end of 1979, several former members of the ERP travelled to Paraguay to locate Somoza´s house in Asunción and collect data on his daily routine, a mission that was carried out very carefully, without the Paraguayan police ever suspecting that an operation was being mounted to kill the former Nicaraguan president. The code name for the attack was Operation Reptile, while Somoza was given the code name Eduardo. Other members of the group joined later, and the team eventually numbered four men and three women: Enrique Haroldo Gorriarán Merlo (alias Ramón), Hugo Alfredo Irurzún (Capitán Santiago), Roberto Sánchez (Armando), Juan José Pandinni (Osvaldo), Silvia Mercedes Hodgers (Teniente Hilda/Diana/Julia), Claudia Benetti Diapo (Susana) and Olga Silvia Avila Cuello (Ana). Many years later, Roberto Sánchez said during an interview: "We could not tolerate the existence of millionaire playboys while thousands of Latin Americans died of hunger. We were perfectly willing to give our lives for that cause."

Since Somoza's departures and schedules were not regular, it was difficult to plan

Argentinian ERP (People's Revolutionary Army) led by Enrique Gorriarán Merlo, in conjunction with Sandinista authorities, were planning the assassination of the former Nicaraguan dictator. Several members of the ERP had been directly involved in the

an ambush. It was also very difficult to follow him without raising suspicions from the Paraguayan police. The guerrillas discussed options for an espionage strategy that would not attract anyone's attention, and thus the idea arose of proposing to the owner of a

Asesinaron a Somoza

El ex—presidente de Nicaragua cayó víctima de ráfagas de ametralladora y del impacto directo de una granada de bazooka que explotó en el asiento delantero de su coche particular, en momentos en que el vehículo se desplazaba por la Avda. España, entre las calles Venezuela y América. El atentado ocurrió a las 9:55 y habrían participado del operativo seis terroristas extranjeros, según versiones, todos ellos están prófugos y uno presumiblemente resultó herido en la balacera. Murieron también dos acompañantes del Gral. Somoza: su asistente, el Sr. Jou Baittiner, de nacionalidad colombiana, y el chofer César Gallardo, nicaragüense. Se ha montado un vasto operativo policial y militar para detener a los terroristas y existe un rígido control en todos los puestos fronterizos, mientras que ayer fueron suspendidos los vuelos comerciales. La Policía ofrece una recompensa de cinco millones de guaraníes a quien brinde pistas de los autores del atentado, entre los cuales estarían Hugo Alfredo Yrurzun y Silvia Mercedes Hodgers, ambos del Ejército Revolucionario del Pueblo (ERP), de Argentina. (Págs. 12, 13, 14, 15, 16, 17 y 18)

JUEVES, 18 DE SETIEMBRE DE 1981
Gs. 15 - 88 PAGINAS - AÑO 14 - Nº 4767

COLOR abc

UN DIARIO JOVEN CON FE EN LA PATRIA
ASUNCION-PARAGUAY

En la foto de arriba puede apreciarse el estado en que quedó el Mercedes Benz del Gral. Somoza después de recibir los impactos de bala y de la granada que estalló en el asiento delantero, destruyendo el techo del vehículo. La fuerza de la explosión levantó al chofer y lo lanzó al pavimento a varios metros de donde fue a quedar el rodado. En la foto de abajo un primer plano del coche. Las mantas amarillas cubren los cadáveres de Somoza y de su asistente, el Sr. Baittiner. A la izquierda, el ex presidente nicaragüense, en oportunidad de la reunión de prensa que ofreció en nuestro país el 22 de agosto del año pasado, tres días después de haber llegado a Asunción. Sus restos son velados en la casa de las calles Gral. Genes y Kasianoff, donde residía últimamente. No se determinó aún dónde serán inhumados. Se estima que su hijo Anastasio, así como otros familiares, arribaría hoy procedente de los Estados Unidos.

The front cover of the Paraguayan *ABC Color* newspaper the day after the attack on Somoza. (*ABC Color*)

The house the ERP guerillas rented on Generalissimo Franco Avenue in Asunción, from where the attack was launched. On the pavement is the corpse of César Gallardo, Somoza's driver. (Diario Ultima Hora)

Military and police personnel in the streets of Asunción during the operation mounted to capture those involved in the attack. (*ABC Color* & Ultima Hora)

the centre of Asunción, along Generalissimo Franco Avenue. They also discovered that he frequented certain restaurants and it was hoped to carry out the attack when he was having lunch or dinner in one of them, but that was thought to be too risky as there was no certainty of achieving their objective.

On 15 September 1980, two days before the attack, the group distributed the weapons and designated the roles to be played during the operation. Armando received one of the Ingram MC-10 machine guns, while Ramón had an M16 rifle and Browning 9mm pistol, and Captain Santiago was given charge of the RPG-7. Osvaldo would be at the newsstand with a walkie-talkie to inform the group that the target was in sight, Armando would be driving the Chevrolet C-10 to intercept the convoy and Captain Santiago would be in the garden of the house on Generalissimo Franco Avenue aiming at Somoza's car with the RPG-7 with Ramón. It was decided that the women of the group would not participate in the attack.

magazine and newspaper stand on Generalissimo Franco Avenue to 'invest' in his business to enlarge it. The owner accepted without asking questions as he wished to get the better of a competitor's magazine stand that was in front of his. The seven-strong group of terrorists also rented a house on the same street since Somoza's car and his escort always used it to travel into downtown Asunción. As it was an exclusive neighbourhood and the luxurious houses were not rented to just anyone, the guerrillas made up a story that the popular Spanish singer Julio Iglesias was coming to Paraguay to work on a movie and for several recitals, and wanted to stay in a house rather than a hotel. One of the guerrilla's women posed as the representative of Iglesias and showed a false document from the Association of Argentine Artists to add credibility to the story.

The logistics were now in place for the attack, including the weapons that were to be used. The group had a Chinese RPG-7 grenade launcher with four anti-tank grenades and two rockets, two Ingram MC-10 machine guns, an M16 rifle and two Browning 9mm pistols. The weapons had been shipped from Nicaragua to Argentina and then moved clandestinely across the Paraná River into Paraguay, using small boats owned by people who were engaged in smuggling activities. The guerrillas also bought an old Chevrolet C10 pick-up truck for the operation and their escape from the scene of the attack.

The guerrillas carefully studied Somoza's movements through Asunción for several months. They realised that an ambush was going to be difficult to carry out as his movements were very irregular, although sometimes he would take the same route towards

On 17 September, Somoza used the white, unarmoured Mercedes-Benz S-Class with Asunción license plates. That day, Somoza was in the rear seats with his financial adviser, Italian-American Joseph Baittiner, who had arrived in Paraguay just the day before, and the driver was César Gallardo. Somoza ordered his police escort to follow him in another car. Commissioner González used his own vehicle, a Ford Corcel II, as the police's red Ford Falcon had mechanical problems. The police officers all had 9mm pistols, and one of them was carrying a Beretta 9mm submachine gun. The escort was composed of Police Commissioner González, 1st Officer Juan Manuel Frutos, 2nd Officer Esteban Marino Venialgo and Assistant Officer Bienvenido Melgarejo. The destination that day was an American bank in the heart of Asunción, where Somoza was to make an important money transfer. They all left the house and drove along Generalissimo Franco Avenue. At 10:35 a.m., Osvaldo spotted the convoy and transmitted the agreed signal to his accomplices: "Target in sight. Get ready."

As per their plan, Ramón stationed himself with his M16 in the garden of the house, while Armando left in the Chevrolet pick-up truck to intercept Somoza's motorcade. Somoza's Mercedes was about 100 metres away, stopped by a red traffic signal, behind six other vehicles. When the traffic light turned green, Armando calculated the time to let about three vehicles pass and then intercept the Mercedes, while Ramón gave the signal to Santiago to have the grenade launcher ready. Armando then burst into the street with the Chevrolet, forcing a Volkswagen Kombi to stop, with Somoza's car behind it. Meanwhile, Santiago was having problems with the RPG-7, which misfired, so Ramón made a swift decision to jump over the garden fence and go directly to the Mercedes. He opened fire with his M16, first killing the driver and then the other two occupants in the rear seats. After he walked calmly away, Santiago reloaded the RPG-7, aimed and fired. The projectile hit the cabin of the Mercedes and the massive explosion destroyed one of the front doors and the roof of the car; the corpse of the driver ended up several metres in front of the vehicle, decapitated and without arms. The other two victims, Somoza and Baittiner, were in the back seat, burned and disfigured. While all this was happening, Somoza's police escort opened fired on the guerrillas, but were unable to hit any of them. The ambush had been a complete success: the 54-year-old Somoza was dead.

Once the attack was over, the four guerrillas got into the Chevrolet truck and escaped down America Street but had to abandon the vehicle just a few blocks away due to mechanical problems. They then separated, using different routes to make their escape. All except Santiago got away safely, making it in disguise either to Argentina or Brazil. Santiago first went to the house they rented in the San Vicente neighbourhood to collect some money, around US$4,000, and the rest of the group's weapons. This deviation from the original plan proved fatal for him, as he was spotted by police, chased and wounded in the ankle. The police surrounded the property and captured him, taking him to the Investigation Department. He was subjected to savage torture to reveal information about his companions and was later shot and killed.

Just minutes after the attack, a large number of police personnel, led by the Minister of the Interior himself, Sabino Augusto Montanaro, Chief of Police, General Alcibiades Brítez Borges and Chief of the Investigation Department Pastor Coronel were on the scene. A police firefighter company retrieved the charred bodies from the wreckage and cleared up the scene, but not before this was witnessed by Somoza's lover, Dinorah Sampson.

An enormous police and military operation was immediately mounted to catch those responsible for the attack, encompassing the whole country. The borders were closed and everyone trying to leave through the international airport was checked, but all to no avail, the remaining six members of the ERP eluding capture and making good their escape. The operation to capture the attackers continued for six months. For several weeks, Army patrols established checkpoints in different parts of the capital and around the interior of the country, while police units raided the homes of people who were suspected, mainly Argentines living in Paraguay. Many people were arrested for not having the correct identity documents. However, the police were not able to come up with the expected results, so they instead focused on scapegoats, arresting many innocent people, including the owner of the house rented to the terrorists, the engineer Alberto Montero de Vargas, and Commissioner González himself due to his inability to protect Somoza. The Chilean photographer Alejandro Mella Latorre, who had worked for the Somoza regime in Nicaragua and was suspected of having collaborated with the Sandinistas, was also arrested. The Chief of Investigations, Pastor Coronel, pressured Commissioner González to testify against Latorre, but he refused and was consequently discharged from the police and held under arrest for 14 months.

Somoza's dismembered body was put back together by doctors in a hospital in Asunción, after which his coffin was transported to Miami in the United States to be placed in the crypt of the Somoza Portocarrero family. His funeral was attended by numerous Nicaraguan exiles in the US, several sympathisers, his widow Mrs Hope Portocarrero – a US citizen – and her children, and even Somoza's mother. The former dictator's lover also went to Miami, where she lived in an apartment that Somoza had given her. Needless to say, Somoza's death caused immense joy in the Sandinistas' ranks and among their followers in Nicaragua. A *Radio Sandino* broadcast stated that 17 September, the day of the execution of Somoza, who was responsible for the deaths of more than 100,000 Nicaraguans and plunged the country into misery, was to be a national day of celebration.

CONCLUSION

The first two guerrilla movements described in this book failed in their fight against the regime of General Stroessner. Neither of them was able to establish secure bases of support among the population and as a result, they were quickly eliminated. Its few surviving members have stated that the lack of planning and coordination were decisive for their catastrophic outcome.

A string of errors led the guerrillas to the most terrible defeat: they did not have control of the territory, orders and counter-orders were followed with total inexperience, communications did not work and there was no unity of command between both guerrilla factions. In addition, as already mentioned, there were government agents infiltrated in both guerrilla groups, so the authorities knew in advance about their plans.

Although the majority of the members of both groups had the will to fight against what they considered a dictatorship, they did not have the necessary military training and were undisciplined. Their leaders were irresponsible and even self-centred, and the guerrillas were too naïve in just trying to copy the Cuban Revolution, without considering the great differences that existed between the situation in Cuba and Paraguay.

On the other hand, the success of the Stroessner regime in the fight against the insurgents was fundamentally due to a very effective system of repression, the support of the American government and the use of nationalistic ideology. The repressive government system was the key to maintaining control over the general population. Unlike other countries in South America, Paraguay did not have parallel police units, clandestine militias and clandestine detention centres, but rather all the repression was carried out by regular police and military forces, and the detention centres were the police stations themselves and military bases. The intelligence centre for the Stroessner regime was the National Directorate for Technical Affairs (*Dirección Nacional de Asuntos Técnicos*, DNAT) of the Police Investigation Department. The US government supported the creation of the DNAT at the time, under the advice of US Army Colonel Robert K. Thierry, a Korean War veteran, who was an expert in military intelligence and counterinsurgency. The DNAT's director, Dr Antonio Campos Alúm, served as the Stroessner government's liaison with the CIA and FBI to exchange vital information. He had been trained in the anti-subversive fight in the United States in 1957. The DNAT consisted of an extensive network of informants, who were engaged in regular surveillance of the activities of opponents of the regime. Those informants, in essence internal spies and known as *pyragüés* in the native Guaraní language, were in the public administration, the diplomatic service and the various Colorado Party premises. It was no coincidence that those spies had infiltrated the ranks of both guerrilla groups, the M14-V and FULNA. Thus, the government learned of all their plans in advance. The repression was extended not only to those involved in the armed struggle against the regime but also to their relatives and friends, who were arrested, interrogated and often tortured to obtain information on the insurgents. The Stroessner government received a major flow of information from the CIA on the political and military contacts of both the M14-V and FULNA in Buenos Aires, Havana and Caracas, which was channelled through the DNAT.

The resounding failure of both guerrilla movements consolidated the Stroessner regime, and although there was one more attempt in 1976 with a socialist group called the *Organización Político-Militar* (OPM, Political-Military Organization), which wanted to organise a cell for a future urban guerrilla uprising, its members were captured and tortured by the police. Many of them died in prison. In 1980, the last huge repression of the regime took place when the police arrested numerous farmers.

Once the guerrilla movements had been defeated, the military justice system, in order to justify the excesses against prisoners, appealed to Decree-Law Nr. 6433 of 18 December 1944, which contemplated exemplary punishment for political-military crimes. Under this law, those who made attempts on the life of the President of the Republic, ministers of state, military and police commanders could be punished with 10–20 years of military confinement, and if the victim of the attack died, the author or authors would suffer the death penalty. For such cases, martial law was employed.

Despite the leaders of the traditional opposition parties in Paraguay distancing themselves from these subversive groups, their own scope for action was increasingly reduced. The Stroessner regime maintained a tiny opposition in parliament, so that in the eyes of the world, Paraguay was seen as a democratic country where opponents could carry out party political activities and be members of parliament.

With regards to foreign policy, Paraguay was distancing itself from Argentina and moving closer to Brazil, but in the mid-1970s, the military regimes in Argentina, Bolivia, Uruguay, Brazil, Chile and Paraguay worked in coordination to capture and extradite not only members of the radical opposition but also potential subversive leaders. This coordinated action was widely known as Operation Condor.

Many people who were against the military regimes – intellectuals, politicians, university professors and students, professionals, Catholic priests and nuns, etc. – were kidnapped, many of them simply disappearing. They were not only arrested and extradited, but tortured and most of them murdered, especially in Chile and Argentina, with smaller numbers in other countries. In Paraguay, there was a huge wave of repression between 1974 and 1976, starting with the first attempt to kill President Stroessner by a group led by Dr Agustín Goiburú – which was thwarted by the regime's security forces – and the attempt to form the OPM urban guerrilla group. All those involved were captured, tortured and then 'disappeared'. Troops led by Paraguayan Army Colonel Grau also captured many farmers who were organised in a group known as the *Ligas Agrarias* (Agrarian Leagues), suspected of being communist cells.

The final attempt at an armed struggle, although not aiming to seize power but just to protest against injustice, was the Caaguazú Case, which ended in a massacre in March 1980. A few months later, a terrorist attack planned by members of the Argentine ERP group assassinated former Nicaraguan dictator Anastasio Somoza Debayle in Asunción.

BIBLIOGRAPHY

Arce Farina, José, *Las Fuerzas Armadas y el Stronismo*, Colección 60 años del Stronismo (Asunción: Editorial El Lector, 2014)

Bejarano, Colonel DEM Ramón C., *Contribución de las FF.AA. al bienestar y progreso del país* (Asunción: Editorial Toledo, 1959)

Boccia Paz, Dr Alfredo, *Goiburú. La odisea del insumiso* (Asunción: Editorial Servilibro, 2014)

Cortese, Vicealmirante César E., *Comunismo: Ideología y Expansión. Anexo C: Intentos del comunismo en el Paraguay* (Asunción, Revista Naval Nro. 113, 1985)

Duré, Víctor & Silva, Agripino, 'Frente Unido de Liberación Nacional (1959–1965), guerra de guerrillas como guerra del pueblo', *Novapolis, Revista Paraguaya de Estudios Políticos Contemporáneos*, www.pyglobal.com (2004)

Ehlers, Hartmut, 'The Paraguayan Navy Past & Present, Part III', *Warship International*, No. 2 (Bexhill-on-sea, UK, 2007)

English, Adrian, *The Paraguayan Army: An outline history* (Dublin: unpublished, 2018)

Lachi, Marcelo *et al.*, *Insurgentes. La Resistencia armada a la dictadura de Stroessner*, Colección Novapolis (Asunción: Editorial Arandurá, 2004)

McQuilkin, Christopher R., 'An excellent laboratory: U.S. foreign aid in Paraguay, 1942–1954', thesis presented to the Department of History and Graduate School of the University of Oregon (September 2014)

Memorandum of a conversation, Department of State, Washington, on Paraguayan purchase of 20 AT-6G planes (18 November 1955)

Miranda, Aníbal, *EE.UU. y el Régimen Militar Paraguayo (1954–1958)* (Asunción: Editorial El Lector, 1987)

Miranda, Anibal, *United States-Paraguay Relations: The Eisenhower Years* (Washington DC: Latin American Program, The Wilson Center, Smithsonian Institution, 1990)

Montero, Mariano Damián, *Agapito Valiente. Stroessner Kyhujeha* (Asunción: Editorial Arandurá, 2019)

Mora, Frank O. & Cooney, Jerry W., *El Paraguay y Estados Unidos* (Asunción: Ed. Intercontinental, 2009)

Nickson, Andrew, *La Guerra Fría y el Paraguay* (Asunción: Colección 60 años del Stronismo, Editorial El Lector, 2014)

Nickson, Andrew, *Las Guerrillas del Alto Paraná* (Asunción: Colección Guerras y Violencia Política en el Paraguay, Volumen 16, Editorial El Lector, 2013)

Nickson, Andrew, *Oscar Creydt* (Asunción: Colección Protagonistas de la Historia, Editorial El Lector, 2011)

Olmedo, Colonel DEM Agustín, *Historia del Colegio Militar Mcal. Francisco Solano López, 1915–1985*, Volumes I and II (Asunción: Imprenta Militar, 1990/92)

Public Record Office, Document FO371/120508-112736, Confidential Dispatch No. 7 with secret enclosure 1381/2/56G, British Embassy, Asunción, Paraguay, 18 January 1956, on the annual report on the Paraguayan Army Air Force

Rivarola, Milda, *La resistencia armada al stronismo* (Asunción: Colección 60 años del Stronismo, Volumen 7, Editorial El Lector, 2014)

Rivalora, Milda, *Letras de Sangre. Diarios inéditos de la Contrainsurgencia y la Guerrilla (Paraguay, 1960)* (Asunción: Editorial Servilibro, 2012)

Sapienza Fracchia, Antonio Luis, *Fuerza Aérea Paraguaya. Historia Ilustrada, 1913–2013* (Asunción: Fuerza Aérea Paraguaya, 2013)

Sapienza Fracchia, Antonio Luis, "Historia Gráfica de la Aviación Naval Paraguaya, 1929–2019. 90 años al servicio de la Patria" (Asunción: Editorial Arandurá, 2019)

Sapienza Fracchia, Antonio Luis, *La Historia de Líneas Aéreas Paraguayas* (Asunción: author's edition, 2004)

USAF Intelligence Report Nr. AF474738/IR-20-53 dated 15 February 1953 on an ex-TWA DC-3 delivered to the Paraguayan Air Force

USAF Intelligence Report Nr. AF677333/IR-155-55 dated 1 August 1955 on the totals of aircraft on hand with the FAP

USAF Intelligence Report Nr. AF714820/IR-9-56 dated 7 December 1955, by LTC Vergil N. Nestor, covering FAP AOB

Ynsfrán, Edgar L., *Memorias* (Asunción: Tomo II, Fundación Ymaguaré de Imágenes y Libros del Paraguay, Editorial Arandurá, 2015)

Zub Centeno, Mónica, *Somoza en Paraguay. Vida y muerte de un dictador* (Asunción: Editorial El Lector S.A., 2014)

ABOUT THE AUTHOR

Antonio Luis Sapienza Fracchia was born in Asunción, Paraguay on 14 May 1960. He graduated from the Catholic University of Asunción with a BA in Clinical Psychology. He also took specialised English courses at Tulane University of New Orleans, Louisiana, USA, and San Diego State University in California. He is now retired but worked for nearly 40 years as an English teacher and one of the Academic Coordinators at the Centro Cultural Paraguayo-Americano (CCPA), a binational institute in Asunción. Married with two children, he resides in the capital. He is an aviation historian who has written more than 500 articles in specialised magazines and web pages on the Paraguayan Aviation history, and has given numerous lectures in schools, universities, institutes and military and civil institutions in Paraguay and abroad. Since 2010, he has been an aviation history professor in the Paraguayan Air Force (FAP). He has published 17 books since 1996, this one being his fifth with Helion. He has received a total of six decorations for his academic merits: two from Argentina, one from Brazil and three from his native Paraguay.